Published by 404 Ink Limited
www.404Ink.com
hello@404ink.com

All rights reserved © layla-roxanne hill & Francesca Sobande, 2025.

The rights of layla-roxanne hill & Francesca Sobande to be identified as the Authors of this Work has been asserted in accordance with the Copyright, Designs and Patent Act 1988.

All rights reserved. No part of this publication may be: i) reproduced or transmitted in any form, electronic or mechanical, including photo-copying, recording or by means of any information storage or retrieval system without prior permission in writing from the publishers; or ii) used or reproduced in any way for the training, development or operation of artificial intelligence (AI) technologies, including generative AI technologies. The rights holders expressly reserve this publication from the text and data mining exception as per Article 4(3) of the Digital Single Market Directive (EU) 2019/790

Please note: Some references include URLs which may change or be unavailable after publication of this book. All references within endnotes were accessible and accurate as of December 2024 but may experience link rot from there on in.

Editing: Laura Jones-Rivera
Proofreading: Heather McDaid
Typesetting: Laura Jones-Rivera
Cover design: Luke Bird
Co-founders and publishers of 404 Ink:
Heather McDaid & Laura Jones-Rivera

Print ISBN: 978-1-916637-06-1
Ebook ISBN: 978-1-916637-07-8

Printed and bound in Great Britain by Clays Ltd, Elcograf S.p.A.

404 Ink acknowledges and is thankful for support from Creative Scotland in the publication of this title.

LOTTERY FUNDED

Look, Don't Touch

Reflections on the Freedom to Feel

layla-roxanne hill
Francesca Sobande

Inklings

Contents

Introduction
On Tenderness and Touch   1

Chapter 1
Holding Space: On Holding and Being Held   8

Chapter 2
I'm Not Okay: On Emotions and Monsters   30

Chapter 3
Feeling Music and Movies: On Materiality,
Moons, and Myths   43

Chapter 4
Something is Off/Online: On Social Media
Spectacle and Digital Life   66

Conclusion
Windows, Wanders/Wonders, and (Wild)flowers   91

Playlist   104
References   111
Acknowledgements   119
About the Authors   121
About the Inklings series   122

Introduction
On Tenderness and Touch

Volcanoes erupt and so do people. Understandably, we're told to fear volcanic eruptions. But beyond the dangers they pose is a powerful process of pressure release. The word "erupt" is associated with dramatic and violent (out)bursts of activity: an uncontrollable explosiveness and catastrophic effects. Volcanic eruptions can bring disaster and devastation, yet many different forms of release are natural and needed. This means that the term "erupt" can also conjure up gentler associations with catharsis and refusing repression – a helpful (even, *healing*) heat, not always a harmful one. Emotional "eruptions" can clear space to process feelings and tend to tension. In a sense they can bring relief as well as chaos: times that may be both tender and tough.

One person's concept of abrupt eruption may be another's step towards liberation. When someone punctures suppressive silence(s) by challenging abuse, they may be supported by some people but scorned by others. The related labels of "breakdown" and "meltdown" are often used to undermine people impacted by traumatic experiences of home(s), education, work, family, loss, and care systems. Depending on their use, "breakdown" and "meltdown" can be careless, cruel, and ableist terms. Surrounding them is the stigma of being (seen as) mentally and/or physically unwell, plus pressures to "get well soon" and "put yourself back together (again)".

Labelling responses to abuse, pain, trauma, and grief as "breakdowns" or "meltdowns" can callously (re)frame people as little more than jagged and jarring. This denies the personal and structural conditions that can lead to someone saying or doing something deemed disruptive. Society quickly writes people off as "unstable", failing to hold the wholeness of who they are, or to address circumstances that lead to someone moving through the world in so-called "unacceptable" ways. What would happen if instead of being dismissed, such people were embraced, *fully*?

Originating from an old English proverb about children, the saying "Should be seen and not heard" is one of countless that signal society's obsession with shutting people down/out. To draw on a Scottish expression, people are constantly told to "haud yer wheesht!" (be quiet!). Public messaging, media, and street signage often pushes the idea of keeping up appearances, being quiet, and focusing on yourself, rather than truly connecting with others. Exceptions to this (see the image on the next page for an example*) can be a shining light, but the need for them is still a concerning sign of isolation in society.

"No Busking. This is a residential area" sign in London, October 2024. Photograph by Francesca Sobande

---

* The bench in the image on the next page was placed in Bute Park in Cardiff (Wales), after author Allison Owen-Jones campaigned to try to tackle societal loneliness and isolation. After encountering an elderly man who was barely acknowledged by anyone when spending much time on a park bench in Cardiff, Owen-Jones came up with the idea for the "Happy to chat" bench. Similar initiatives exist elsewhere too.

"Whose eyes are on your phone?
Take care, don't lose it" sign in London, October 2024.
Photograph by Francesca Sobande

"Sit here if you don't mind someone stopping to say hello / Eisteddwch yma os ydych yn hapus i rywun stopio i ddweud helo" bench in Cardiff, November 2024.
Photograph by Francesca Sobande

Many social "rules" are enforced daily, but life is unpredictable, so *Look, Don't Touch* embraces spontaneity, release, messiness, and softness. Indeed, in these mid-2020s, "softness" is having a moment. There is so much #SoftLife social media content, on everything from "wellness" and "financial independence" to "cottagecore" and "nomadic travel/work". In shops, soft furnishings foster fantasies of homeliness. In editorials, the "softboy/boi" qualities of famous men are hailed as "modern" masculinities – usually without addressing power dynamics that impact who is perceived and praised as soft.

Don't get us wrong, we're here for softness and enjoy *lots* of music, materials, and moments described as "soft". But we're also critical of when softness is (re)presented as a hyper-visible trend and luxurious (middle-class) aspiration. Softness is somehow everywhere and nowhere. It's promoted via commodities, services, and touristic narratives of the grass being greener over there, where if you have the money, time, and rights, you can go (and *maybe*, stay). That said, our book affirms softness, just not consumerist illusions of it. So, before we take our time to turn to tenderness and touch, we'll sit with softness too – naming some of the contradictions that can be part of desire(s), connection, intimacy, and care. Softness is nothing if not layered.

Embracing the strength of softness is key to experiences of tenderness and love. Yet so too is dealing with discomfort: expressing that you miss someone, deeply mourning, working through friction, accepting change, acknowledging difference, and feeling the intensity of remembrance. You could say that this means softness can also be something that's very hard. It's never a given. Instead, softness is a precious possibility and practice – tending to yourself and each other. There is softness in vulnerability – choosing to be open with another soul: holding and being held, moving from longing to loving. Softness is truly found in glimmers of stillness, connections and movements that are far removed from a fixation on money, materialism, or the constant cycle of buzzy media. Softness can be freeing.

If anchored in an anti-imperialist position that addresses class, gender, racial, sexual, and disability politics, softness can be a bold statement put into action. It can be at the core of efforts to push back against vicious governments and those who seek to suppress love, life, and liberation. Softness is caring. It's never just about a tactile texture or something visible. It's as much about interior convictions and shared struggles as it is about how they are (not) externally expressed. From the tangible to the sensual – softness is, first and foremost, *felt*.

Throughout history, lots of words have been used to express what feelings are. Rather than just turning to words, we want to make time and space for music and images too. So, a playlist accompanies our book and visuals feature in it. While *Look, Don't Touch* considers some of the different perspectives of people, we also focus on paws/pause for thought – inspired by time with animals and different species (including each of our dugs foxi and Ez).

As we continue to reflect on, softness and connected feelings and encounters such as tenderness, dreaming, and love aren't simply about what is expressed to others. They are also about what is felt and acknowledged within and for (y)ourselves. People shouldn't have to excavate their life story to "prove" they're "deserving" of softness, tenderness, dreaming, and love. Even so, an openness to being held means figuring out how to connect to and through each other's perspectives and experiences.

Accordingly, the references in our book echo elements of our experiences of ADHD/neurodivergence, and our intention to avoid masking in/through writing. The thoughts and feelings expressed in the chapters that follow are far from linear and your approach to reading them doesn't need to be either. Feel free to journey to or with our book in whatever way feels best, whether that's turning to a random page, starting at the back of it, doodling in/on it, or moving towards the playlist before checking out our words and images. Please take the time you want and need to be with (or away from) our sharing. After all, we hope you feel forms of freedom in how you experience *Look, Don't Touch*, and in how you experience life.

Chapter 1
Holding Space: On Holding and Being Held

I'm by your side
A problem shared…
Need a shoulder?
Your secret is safe…
Spoon me?

There are infinite ways to share desires to be held and to convey you(r) care for another: a dug's nose nuzzling for a reassuring touch; the cry of a baby calling for a soothing cradling; a friend's outstretched arms, welcoming a heart-felt hug; the indescribable feeling of cwtch/cwtsh, the peace of sleeping in, and the bliss of getting cooried into comforting spaces or into each other. What is life if not reaching for another, even, and *especially*, in times of vulnerability. Away from such moments of intimacy, people encounter expectations of (with)holding – "stiff upper lip" messages and cues to act cool/standoffish by turning away from tenderness. Still, connection can prevail.

For example, there are clear forms of connection in shared values (equity, justice, care) that bring and hold people and communities together. Connection can also be moulded by music. As Laina Dawes puts it in the 2012 book, *What Are You Doing Here?: A Black Woman's Life and Liberation in Heavy Metal*: "Songs create an emotional bond between a sound and the listener...We identify with a particular song, or a sound, or an entire genre of music, and suddenly we feel less alone."[1] In the words of the endearing character Jody in Nate Powell's graphic novel *Fall Through*, about an underground punk band in a time loop, "[m]usic has bound me to the people I love."[2] As has influenced *Look, Don't Touch*, music is part of who and how we love (and are loved), as well as being part of who and how we are.

Connectedness is also found in how physical structures are imagined, designed, and sustained, including in ways that support many species and their different needs. At its crux, connection involves *creating*, whether by carefully crafting the architecture of a space, or by trying to relate to someone in ways that surpass the superficial – relationships rooted in more than assumptions and idealisation, and building(s) based on possibilities not mere practicalities. Such a spirit of connection means forging and nurturing bonds with care, courage, and commitment. It means being vulnerable and viscous – open to change, rather than regulated and rigid.

Webs of/as Connection

As something fragile and formidable – a fleeting formation and a fraying force – a spider's web symbolises connection. The fear of spiders (termed arachnophobia) is one of the most common phobias. Yet, having existed for at least 300 million years, spiders are part of the fabric of the world. This is their home too, not just "ours". For these reasons, and more, much can be learnt from spiders and their movements on this earth.

Often portrayed as a creepy nuisance – hence the moniker "creepy crawly" – spiders are regularly invoked as symbols of eerie occurrences. But the meanings and moods ascribed to spiders are culturally specific. For example, in West African mythology and folklore (such as the Akan tale of Anansi, the spider-man of Ghana), spiders are connected to wisdom and a trickery that may disrupt, but not always disturb. Anansi was part of the inspiration behind the name of British rock band Skunk Anansie, fronted by Skin, who as a child saw a Jamaican cartoon about the character. That's just one of many examples of how spiders and storytelling about them shape music.

Jennifer Osakpolor Irabor, an Irish-Nigerian artist and musician known as SPIDER, captures many of these meanings and moods as she spins threads of pop punk, emo and grunge into themes of emotions (and the fullness of them), vulnerability, astrology, sex, and sexuality. SPIDER says of getting into music, "I didn't get into music to improve, you know what I mean? …I got into it to express myself and to make things the way I want to, and so I was just like, 'Fuck it'."[3]

Released in 2023, the music video for "AMERICA'S NEXT TOP MODEL" shows SPIDER confronted by six agressive white men, who she faces both individually and, at times, surrounded by them, each shouting and pointing at her, reflecting online and offline responses to Black women being part of – and making music in – "alternative" scenes. As SPIDER moves and dances amongst the men freely, questioning why they are scared, it's as though the men are stuck in a web-like structure, unable to shift their way of thinking to be free. SPIDER disrupts, (re)claims being punk, and shows the viewer that it's the men who don't want to give up, share or hold space who are frightened, not her.

Much like SPIDER's music, delicate in its details but bold in its building, a spider's web can have a strong and shimmering sense of serenity, combined with an inescapable feeling of friction that frames certain times in life. In essence, a spider's web reflects connectedness and the power and precariousness that prop it up. Rather than being something to be swept away – as the expression "dust off the cobwebs" suggests, we view such webs as wondrous weavings to be celebrated.

A spider's web, 2024. Photograph by Francesca Sobande

Consisting of complex connections, a spider's web is a structure that can embody the continuum of life and death, making for moments of pause as you pass one and notice what is (or isn't) caught in it. Central to how spiders feed and fend for themselves, their webs aren't for show. They're a space and source of sustenance – both a home and a holding: a spider's safety and a trap to others. Recognising all this is important when treating certain connections in ways that aren't simplified, and in ways that don't treat life and death as diametric opposites.

Stating that doesn't diminish the gravity of grief and the immeasurable pain of experiencing loss, the depths of which can feel bottomless. We're not suggesting that the entanglements of life and death mean that life and death are the same as each other. Instead, we're acknowledging the many and messy ways that life and death are coupled – two parts of a whole rather than separate experiences that can ever be detached. The existence of one means that of the other, and, so, connectedness is at their shared core.

This means we acknowledge that depending on whose vantage point is focused on – the spider, its prey, or an outside observer – a spider's web can seem helpful and/or harmful. Much like that, connection isn't intrinsically "good" and doesn't neatly result in harmonious interactions, unity, and community. On the contrary, connections can be riddled with moments of conflict, confusion, and contradictions. They can be as frazzled and fraught as fulfilling and feel-good, but they present important potential by bringing and bonding different beings together.

Speaking of spiders, the 1952 book *Charlotte's Web* by E.B. White[4] is perhaps one of the most beloved children's stories, appealing to people of many ages. Both tender and tragic, the book draws readers into a story about kinship, solidarity, and finding meaning in everyday moments. Readers follow a livestock pig named Wilbur, through his bond with an inquisitive barn spider, Charlotte, who tries to save him from being slaughtered. Foregrounding the dearness of friendship, the pain(s) of growing up, and both the full-heartedness and harshness of time passing, *Charlotte's Web* makes sense of what it means to form close connections with others, while knowing (or finding out) that they'll not always (physically) be (t)here.

It's not only spiders, pigs, and their movements that illuminate the intricacies of connection. As the paws/pause for thought sections of *Look, Don't Touch* embrace, every species sheds light on how we all exist in relation to each other and the environment(s) we inhabit. Feeling and being connected to others can be fundamental to forms of freedom. Nevertheless, connection, on its own, is not a magic solution to the world's problems. Then again, webs of care and connection are critical to living and loving in ways that push against pressures to pretend that everything is "okay". This means that care and connection are key to both our present and future.

Connection Needs No Instructions

We, as the world's inhabitants, can't sustain the planet, and more importantly, we can't *transform* it, without a true togetherness that helps to change structural conditions and heal hearts. This means that, no matter how rough and tough it may be to do, we must cultivate connection and care, *always*, and resist isolationist impulses.

Connection doesn't require a manual or commands to call it into being, but we live in a world littered with instructions about who to be and how to behave. When on the phone to an organisation, you may be told to "please hold", before being placed in a queue so long that the phone line eventually disconnects. There are pedestrian signs that symbolise an adult supportively holding a child's hand, but the idea of two adults holding each other's is absent and, even, alien. At some airports there is a time limit on goodbye hugs, treating tenderness as something to be contained. When travelling by train, there may be a mix of messages about being "shhh!" in "the quiet carriage", but also being encouraged to vocally alert someone if "you see something that doesn't look right". As British Transport Police abruptly put it: "See it. Say it. Sorted".

In other words, we're often told who, what, and when (not) to (with)hold.

Beyond being expressed as a blunt directive, throughout history, messages about holding and being held have been taken up in creative ways.

Cry (Like You Mean It), You're on Camera

TV shows such as *Couple's Therapy* (2019–2024) shine a filtered and (un)flattering light on experiences of counselling, catharsis, and crying. The show mixes angular interior aesthetics and direct discussions about the problems and pleasures of partnership, for maximum tense/tender effect. Crying on screen, or anywhere for that matter, shouldn't be stigmatised. But here we are…

Due to inhibiting societal norms (e.g. emotional repression and passive aggression in Britain), many people don't feel free to cry in public. Namely, people impacted by restrictive gendered ideas about emotion and oppressions such as racism, ableism, ageism, classism, homophobia, transphobia, and xenophobia, can face serious repercussions if seen crying. Not all tears elicit (equally) sympathetic responses.

Certainly, crying in public is embraced and even expected in *some* situations and by *some* people. Think tears of sorrow at funerals, and tears of joy at weddings, births, and awards ceremonies. Contrastingly, in other moments, crying is frowned upon, if not forbidden. This reflects how emotions, and their expression, are suppressed – treated as something to compartmentalise and only release in the "right" (read: recognisable, regulated, and restricted) situations/ways.

Crying can mean many different things and be sparked by many different feelings, including, beyond those we discuss, and beyond those that are named in the English language. Similarly, the absence of tears is interpreted in various and culturally dependent ways that relate to different emotions and forms of self-expression. There's more than one way of crying. Crying ≠ just sadness or joy. Not crying ≠ complete happiness or numbness. Regardless of the many feelings that underpin tears rolling, crying tends to be understood as a release, and one often portrayed on screens.

Couple's Therapy provides audiences with a glimpse of the lives of select couples and the work of the therapist(s) they visit. This includes televised representations of people crying while appearing to work through feelings and frictions, under the scrutiny, or with the support, of a camera-ready therapist. Picking up from fictional shows such as *In Treatment* (2008–2021) and memorable portrayals of therapists and psychiatrists in *The Sopranos* (1999–2007) and *Monk* (2002–2009), there has been a burst of TV on real-life therapy, where it's a question of who and when, *not if*, someone cries.

There is nothing wrong with crying. It's a natural experience for many. But cathartic spaces and sources of emotional support involve more than just tears, including by moving away from insular, invasive, and often expensive institutional models of therapy. There is a risk that some popular (pop) culture portrayals of therapy, most of which focus on talking-based approaches, delight in documenting tearfulness. This can (re)establish limiting, and often neurotypical, expectations that people *must* cry (but not too much) to truly (be seen to) access emotional release.

We support efforts to destigmatise crying (as SOPHIE sang, "it's okay to cry"). But this also means being alert to when tearful times are treated as a "look, don't touch" televised moment, not responded to or represented in caring ways.

For the Masses, Not Mass Production

As Joy White affirms in the 2024 book *Like Lockdown Never Happened: Music and Culture During COVID*, "popular culture is one of the ways that we give our lives meaning,"[5] such as by figuring out and expressing our feelings about certain issues. Just as pop culture has continued to play with different portrayals of therapy, there's been an increasing number of therapists stepping into the celebrity and online influencer spotlight, aligned with audience demand for "true life" entertainment media, and intense interest in other people's private pleasures and prickling pains.

Within the genre of "therapy" TV shows is variety, but much of such media focuses on the character(s) of therapists and those who see them, including, in the case of fictional shows, the star image of actors. *Couple's Therapy, In Treatment,* and the dubiously named Netflix series *Gypsy* (2017) depict how some people create, access, and shake up therapeutic space(s). Such media focuses on Western, professionalised, and talking-based therapy, via one-to-one (or in *Couple's Therapy*, one-to-two or more) private appointments. These shows also mainly focus on middle-class people with the money to pay for consistent private counselling, or with a significant salary from their work as a therapist. In sum, depictions of space(s) held in those shows are just a tiny part of a much bigger landscape of how people forge or represent types of care and hold space for/with others.

As R.E.M.'s Michael Stipe poignantly sang, "Everybody hurts… sometimes." Pop culture has a long history of dealing with forms of hurt *and* perpetuating them. Some of this is addressed in the documentary series *Boybands Forever* (2024) which highlights harmful music industry norms. Additionally, a growing number of shows and podcasts have tackled the topic of reality TV and its detrimental impact on many people who are depicted in such media. With all that in mind, it's unsurprising that pop culture has increasingly engaged various ideas associated with therapy and care. That said, rarely does this translate into shifts in the industry, such as proper networks of care for young musicians/bands, or sufficient pre- and post-production care for people on reality TV. Also, some pop culture commentaries on these matters amount to dodgy discourse, empty platitudes, and inane "therapy speak" — catch-all expressions and simplifications of care, used to try to excuse awful actions, rather than to mitigate harm or aid healing.

In that context, the concept of having "boundaries" can become vacuous and vague — a word uttered in defense of selfish, and even, malicious decisions, that are repositioned as (self)caring. As such, across many social media sites is a litany of language and ideas attributed to therapy (often, psychiatry) but much of that really stems from and reframes other perspectives and practices, such as the embodied knowledges of Indigenous people and Black ancestral healing traditions that grow from connectedness and communalism, not individualistic and institutional therapy models. Boundaries aren't about centring one person's preferences or truths over another's. They should be part of our learning how to build communal power and stay in relationship with one another without causing harm to ourselves or each other.

While it's no doubt important to acknowledge and understand different people's experiences of trauma, depression, disability, and ableism, as Vanessa Angélica Villarreal powerfully puts it in 2024's *Magical Realism:*

Essays on Music, Memory, Fantasy, and Borders: "Post-traumatic stress disorder, depression, and ADHD are scientific names for collective narratives, perfectly normal responses to unsurvivable conditions. Trauma is the name individualism gives to a suffering that must stay private, hidden, not part of a collective story."[6] As she points out, unlike the imagined manic pixie (aka "mentally ill", thin, white) dream girl/woman – a staple of 2000s/2010s "indie" pop culture, women of colour "don't get to be fragile, fucked up, or 'crazy' when our labor is the thing that's valuable."[7] In fact, their/our perceived "madness" is usually deemed scary, not enchanting like imagined and off-kilter white women on film.

On that note, while many pop culture portrayals of therapy are lacking in their treatment of feeling(s), we caution against critiques that deify therapy as something pop culture can only corrupt and not reflect. After all, for reasons which include the intersections of racism, sexism, ableism, and capitalism, therapy and the process of pursuing a "diagnosis", and access to care, can be fucked up too!

Therapeutic experiences, cathartic moments, and forms of care should be available to the masses, not treated as a "one size fits all" industry that businesses profit from and some people enact power through. Such spaces must work to address hierarchical dynamics and controlling actions implicated in them, including forms of speciesism[8] that can result in some (often, fluffy) animals (e.g. alpacas, cats, dogs) being treated as nothing more than cute and in service to people as "animal/pet therapy". We're not dismissing the importance of connectedness between species, including humans and other animals. Instead, we're critical of the uncaring and exploitative ways that many people tend to treat certain animals as a source of entertainment or a way to just create comfort for themselves. Why does an animal need to be in service to a human to justify or explain a loving relationship between species?

Undoubtedly, there can be multi-species and communal healing spaces which aren't based on toxic hierarchies between people and different creatures. However, in societies such as the UK and US, where many birds, animals, and insects are treated as means to capitalist and human-centred ends, such spaces are few and far between.

We support *some* of the ways that awareness and critical understanding of forms of therapy and healing have been discussed in different digital spaces. We're also wary of when ideas of therapy and healing have been repurposed as online content churn and "self-help" social media — a chorus of clickbait calls to action ("just tell them…", "sign up for…", "buy this to…", "revisit memories of…") which, for some people, do much more harm than help. Indeed, as White notes on the state of society, "What we cannot escape, though, is the logic of neoliberalism, where individual success and triumphs are highlighted more than institutional and structural inequalities."[9] This results in redundant and self-righteous online instructions on how to do "self-care" right.

Context is key. Intentions behind many people's online posts about therapy and self-help may be less clear-cut than an attempt to gain followers and monetised engagement. Yet even well-meaning posts can feature flippant and depoliticising messages, pushing consumerist ideas about care and holding space, while ignoring structural disparities between people's material conditions and lives.

But *what is* "holding space", anyway?

More than just relating to the idea of active listening,[10] the concept of holding space concerns a range of sources of support, mutuality, and (self)regard. This includes sensitively communicating encouragement, without pressure, to help someone share about themselves and how they're feeling. It can also involve being there for someone and expressing and connecting to them without discussing anything at all.

Essentially, holding space encompasses approaches to caring about the wholeness of each other, such as through relationships that challenge the isolating and crushing nature of capitalism. But discussions about "holding space" often overlook different needs and desires to be held (and to be given space to breathe and just be).

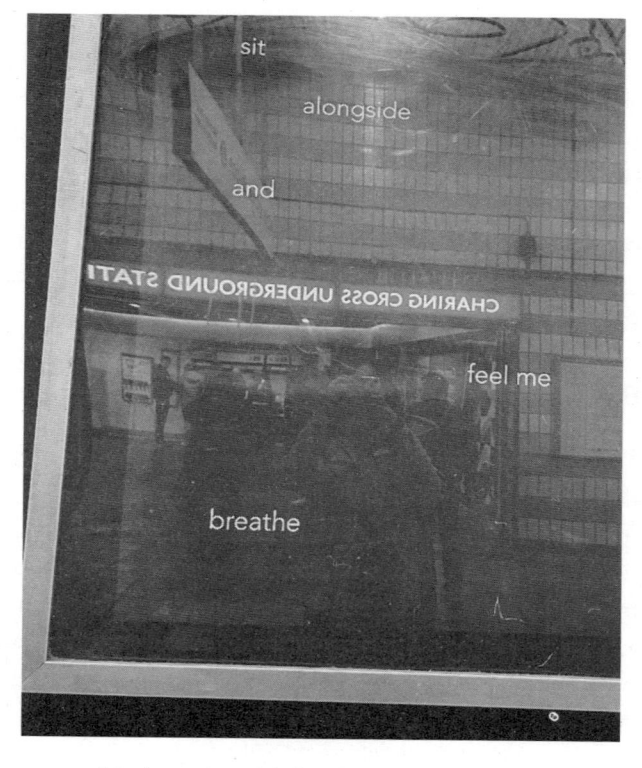

"sit alongside and feel me breathe" public art by Helen Cammock (2021) in London, October 2024. Photograph by Francesca Sobande

There is more than one way to be (t)here for someone else. Access to physical forms of being held is the foundation of some experiences of care, but holding space also means supporting others in different ways. It's about more than being in the same place together at the same time, but that can be a key part of it too.

Holding space can involve being present through asynchronous conversations and connections, such as the paced back and forth of letter writing, the rhythms and revisiting of voice messages, and the expressivity of visual communications. We all need different types of space – a physical form of shelter, space in your mind and heart to engage emotions, a sense of space that comes with reflecting on past experiences, and the outer space that exists beyond the earth's atmosphere. Although the term "holding space" tends to be linked to the desires, needs, and actions of adults, it's important that discussions about it consider and support children's care(s) too.

The Space of Children's TV

Reading Rainbow (1983–2006) was a US public broadcasting service TV programme which celebrated children's books, love of reading, and curiosity. Opening with a catchy and uplifting theme song, the show did much more than hold people's attention for the 30-minute duration of its awe-inspiring episodes. Spanning more than two decades, it held space for children's wants, wonderment, wisdom, and ways of being that were scarcely taken seriously by the media and publishing industries. Fronted by presenter LeVar Burton's warmth, whimsy, and wicked sense of style, *Reading Rainbow* recognised children's feelings, such as their quizzical questions about the world.

Across 21 seasons, the TV show dealt with topics such as love, grief, friendship, being unhoused and displaced, and the impact of a family member being incarcerated. The unique programme provided a space where children could learn about other people's lives or could feel less alone in what they faced. Although it was created before the popularisation of the term "holding space", *Reading Rainbow* is an example of a space that can help children to feel (more) supported and in ways that surpass surface-level media representations or a sole focus on literacy initiatives.

As reflected on in the documentary film, *Butterfly in the Sky* (2022), *Reading Rainbow* and its memorable impact is a form of holding/being held. It's also testament to the work of Burton who, as a Black man in the predominantly white world of children's TV (and, eventually, the outer space of science-fiction TV too!), provided a resonance that particularly bolstered Black children, who are so often underserved by society. However, children's TV is a space where both heartening and harmful experiences exist. The destructive environment that can be part of the production of children's TV has been addressed in numerous documentaries and TV shows. These include *Child Star* and *Quiet on Set: The Dark Side of Kids TV*, as well as the fictional Netflix series *Eric*, all released in 2024.

Set in 1980s New York City, *Eric* portrays the problematics of children's TV and the importance of imagination. It provokes questions about what it means to really be there for a child and to communicate with them in caring ways. The series addresses the harrowing Human Immunodeficiency Virus (HIV)/Acquired Immunodeficiency Syndrome (AIDS) epidemic. Depicting the impact of HIV/AIDS on gay men and people deemed drug "addicts", *Eric* deals with how such individuals are/were demonised and denied forms of holding/being held because of that. As such, even though *Eric* is about how children are (not) cared about/for, it's also about love and care in general, including physical *and* non-physical expressions of that in life and death.

Following a father's quest to find his missing son by bringing to life the child's drawings of a blue monster as a puppet, *Eric* explores society's suppression of creativity and imagination, paired with its punishing and pathologising of people who are labelled little more than "mad", "bad", and/or "sad". As noted in *Land of Change: Stories of Struggle & Solidarity from Wales*, edited by Gemma June Howell, often "working-class lives are portrayed as dysfunctional, dependent on the state and generally a social problem that needs to be solved by the professional middle classes or the philanthropic cultured upper classes."[11] Relatedly, as well as conveying how racism, ableism, colourism, homophobia, transphobia, and capitalism impact which/whose children are discriminated against, *Eric* represents classed pressures that confront parents. These include distinct differences between pressures faced by a Black, working-class, single mother and those faced by white middle-class parents – shaping who is (not) supported by social structures and public institutions (e.g. schools and the police).

In *Eric*, the audience witnesses what happens when a relatively privileged white child's needs are constantly overlooked by busy and bickering adults in their life, who infrequently make time or space to truly be and connect with them. Through its focus on adults searching for missing children, while harking back to the (mis)treatment of adults in their own childhood, *Eric* details how people become perceived as purely a "problem" to "fix", a "madness" to "medicate", or an "issue" to be "institutionalised". Portraying children's TV as trivialised, yet also treated with less contempt than actual children, *Eric* depicts the dangers of aspects of the industry and the broader society it's the outcome of – a society where children are often treated as though they're to be seen, not listened to, unless what they say serves adults' egos.

While the TV show *Reading Rainbow* joyfully put into practice holding space for/with children, *Eric* offers a contrasting commentary on how (some) children are made to feel that they take up too much space and are vilified for (day)dreaming and disabilities. Effectively, *Eric* addresses the grimness of children being disregarded, while *Reading Rainbow* is tenderness in tremendous technicolour.

The space of children's TV remains a significant site of the expression of imagination and emotions, while helping to develop and hold dear the dreams of the next generation(s). However, that space, certainly within public service broadcasting, seems to be narrowing. Examples of that include the end of CITV (the children's strand of Independent Television – a group of British companies that produce TV programmes, paid for by adverts) in 2023, and plans to move CBBC (the children's TV strand of the public service British Broadcasting Corporation) entirely online by 2025. Clearly, much (still) needs to be done to ensure that children can access a wide range of media depictions and discussions created for them, and not just online. It shouldn't need to be said, but children are the future. Let's not only support theirs, but also hold proper space for them in the here and now.

Chapter 2
I'm Not Okay: On Emotions and Monsters

My Chemical Romance at Stadium MK in Milton Keynes, May 2022. Photograph by Francesca Sobande

<3

Emotions are felt and shared. They are chemistry – combustible and cooling. These include emotions expressed through and beyond verbal speech, facial expressions, and body language. This point is conveyed in 2022's *Sensory: Life on the Spectrum – An Autistic Comics Anthology*, edited by artist and curator Bex Ollerton. Bringing together contributions from thirty autistic creators, the anthology addresses different sensory experiences, forms of communicating, and feelings of connection. It's a creation that, with care, deals with the relationship between emotions and all things sensory.

As alluded to in the previous chapter, despite the numerous ways that emotions emerge and are expressed, suggestions to "speak to someone" often dominate discourse about what to do if you don't feel "okay". Rarely does such advice account for the fact that "feeling okay", and the sense of stability associated with it, is not relatable to all. For example, some ideas of "okayness" which frame intense feelings/feeling intensely as nothing but disruptive/destructive, can promote damaging ideas of emotional numbness and dismiss how people really feel – often, "not okay"[12].

Moving Beyond "Okayness"

Dictionaries are a patchy place to start when trying to decode and decipher the details of words and their meanings. At the same time, dictionaries are a source of information about how norms and idea(l)s are expressed through the professed definitions of words. A case in point is what is revealed by looking up "okay" and its claimed origins.

In the online Oxford English Dictionary, the word "okay" is explained with the use of terms such as "satisfactory", "well", "all right", and "all correct". There are also more lukewarm expressions such as "acceptable" and "adequate". Fundamentally, the idea of being okay relates to a sense of "suitability" and "sufficiency". To be okay is not to be glowing or to feel grand, but it's also not to be mired by grimness or ground down in acutely distressing ways. Maybe this makes "okayness" a sort of non-state – a nothingness rather than enoughness. *Are you really "okay"?*

Societies are filled with messages telling you who is, and how to be, okay. In this chapter we question what it means to (not) feel/be okay, when so much is not right in the world – from the genocidal actions of governments to pervasive health inequalities and the many violences of capitalism. How can, and why should, anyone feel "okay" during all of this? This book is not a fatalistic account of life or an advocation for anguish. We aren't disregarding needs and desires to feel and be in ways that involve much more than hollowed out ideas of "wellness" which are pushed by corporations. Instead of rejecting the pursuit of full-hearted feelings – be they intimacy, ecstasy, liberation or peace, we call into question the very idea of "okayness" and its detrimental impacts.

There needs to be much more than the glib refrain that "it's okay not to feel okay", for people to be materially supported in addressing the struggles in their life and the structural causes of them. While recognising the limitations of our own thoughts on all of this, and without framing ourselves as "experts", we consider how certain ideas of "okayness" are constructed and contested. We do this as part of how we think through and with interconnected emotions and experiences that are often treated as conflicting: hope and horror, joy and grief, desire and disgust, and – guided by the work of Lama Rod Owens – *love and rage*.[13]

We share thoughts on this from a place that affirms the vital work of those who encourage young people to express when they don't feel okay. In Cardiff (Wales), this includes Head Above The Waves – an independently run, not-for-profit, mental health organisation, raising awareness of depression and self-harm in young people: "Self-harm affects around 1 in 12 young people, yet it remains an issue people struggle to handle, talk about, and understand. We aim to change this."[14] We also acknowledge the work of Mychal Threets — a US librarian whose viral social media posts and videos include supportive messages for children (and adults) about mental health, reading, and self-expression, which is another testament to the enduring legacy of the spirit of children's TV show *Reading Rainbow* (1993–2006).

As part of our discussion of related matters, we reflect on the societal makings of "madness", including how some notions of "okayness" can be maddening by sustaining a status quo that polices and pathologises people. Before elaborating on the pretense of "okayness" and what may be gained by letting go of it, we focus on the (Black) Gothic — namely, the AMC TV show *Interview with the Vampire*, and its engagements with emotions, the erotic, and (in)sanity. But first, let's talk metal and monsters.

Of Metal and Monsters

While writing *Look, Don't Touch* we watched, listened to, felt, read, reflected on, remixed, released, and returned to many ideas, images, and imaginings. These included representations of gothicness, black metal and nu-metal music, and monsters.

Edited by Daniel Lukes and Stanimir Panayotov in 2023, the collection *black metal rainbows* details the depths and divergences of a music genre/subculture known for its heaviness. Lukes and Panayotov remark that "[s]onically, it can be harsh (it can also be very soft and tender)."[15] When thinking about gothic horror and its atmospheres, we're reminded of such words which relate to how harshness and softness can exist together, wholistically. Much like how black metal is a terrain of both the transgressive and the tender, the gothic can be an outlet for hope and horror.

Based on the influential 1976 book *Interview with the Vampire* by Anne Rice, the gothic horror TV show of the same name (2022–present) has captured hearts, drawing us into the immortal lives of vampires who burn with desire, and some of whom also desire to burn. This is a world where you both love and bite *deeply*.

The writing that led to this show started out as a short story by Rice, which she turned into a book, months after the bereavement of her young daughter. While *Interview with the Vampire* is a gory story, it's also gloriously tender in its treatment of subjects such as intimacy, shame, kinship, "madness", and the raw magnetism of desiring beings who find each other (again and again and again…). Unlike the film *Interview with the Vampire: The Vampire Chronicles* (1994), which was also based on Rice's book, the TV show does not simply skirt around themes of queerness which were part of the original source material. Also, unlike the book, the TV show foregrounds Black queerness, as poignantly explored through the characters of both Louis and Claudia (discussed in more detail later).

Building on the affection and eroticism that is present on the pages of Rice's book, the TV show *Interview with the Vampire* portrays climactic experiences of intimacy, drawing parallels between the referenced idea of "un petit coup" (the little drink [of blood]), and the unspoken but well-known concept of "la petite mort" (the little death) – a French euphemism for post-orgasm. Across two seasons (so far), the show traverses experiences of romance, death, sexuality, race, gender, age(ing), and love. It's an outlandishly enthralling portrayal of beings who are, to draw on the 2005 lyrics of indie band Bloc Party, known for having a "taste for blood".

In an introduction to a 2008 edition of Rice's *Interview with the Vampire*, reflecting on its cultural impact, author Audrey Niffenegger writes: "It's hard to imagine *Buffy the Vampire Slayer* without *Interview with the Vampire*". Expanding on the significance of Rice's tale, Niffenegger claims: "Every era creates the monsters it needs"[16] – society paints certain ideas and people as "evil", "ferocious", and "unknowable" to maintain the power of others who are positioned as "pure", "friendly", and "familiar".

For example, in a crucial account of "The (Un) Changing Nature of Constructions of South Asian

Muslim Women Post-9/11", Maryam Jameela explains, "[o]ne particular figure popular in horror and fantasy genres that use monsters to work through white anxiety is that of ghosts, particularly in relation to how trauma is processed and moved on from. Ghostly apparitions in fiction have a long history of representing a past trauma, or requiring action in order to exercise them and their unfinished business."[17] Similarly, portrayals of vampires can voice such sentiments.

Characters in the TV show *Interview with the Vampire* reflect an amalgamation of monsters needed at the time the book was written (1970s) *and* those conjured up in response to the crises of contemporary times (2020s), including forms of contagion and (lack of) physical intimacy during the COVID-19 pandemic. Society's supposed "monsters" and the stories told about them sometimes serve as a confessional – a conduit through which transgressive desires are reframed as demons to create distance between the monsters and those who can't keep their names out their mouths. To recall the subtitle of the edited collection *True Blood and Philosophy*, about the US vampire drama series *True Blood* (2009–2014): "[w]e wanna think bad things with you."[18] But not everyone is a Vampire Freak.[19]

Be Still, My Beating (Black Gothic Horror) Heart

While Rice's book is the work from which the show sprung, the TV depiction of *Interview with the Vampire* departs from the original text in several ways, such as by rupturing the image of vampires as (all) white and by playing with ideas of multiracial monstrosities, melancholies, and intimacies.

At the centre of the plot is the charming and unreliable narrator, Louis de Pointe du Lac, affectingly played by Jacob Anderson. The blend of the first episode's captivating cinematography, exquisite costumes, moving soundtrack, and otherworldly acting makes for a media experience that is unlike (m)any others. Memorable parts of the script such as "I loved him more than anyone on earth, and our daily stroll to St Augustine was the measure of a good day started" (said by Louis about his brother Paul) return to you often, reminding you of the show's sweetness amid its sharpness, and the many different types of love it dotingly depicts.

Unlike the book and film, in which Louis is a white man and plantation owner, the TV show *Interview with the Vampire* portrays him as a dapper dressed Black Creole man. Louis is brother to Paul (Steven G. Norfleet), who is portrayed as being schizophrenic, suggested by lines of Louis' such as "…Paul confused the dining table with a pulpit that none of us would recognise". An in-depth discussion of how the show treats the topic of (in)sanity and Black "madness" is beyond the scope of our short book. But related depictions in *Interview with the Vampire* include its portrayal of Paul, such as how the show alludes to his ability to sense/see Lestat the Vampire (strikingly played by Sam Reid) for who/what he is. This hints at how very real forms of intuitiveness, connection, and sensing rooted in Black people's embodied ways of knowing are often written off as "madness"/"insanity" and as the opposite of "okay".

Born in the 1870s in New Orleans, Louis cuts a fresh and clean, yet forlorn, figure as he graces the screen. His powerful presence pierces through the noise of busy scenes, and his rousing words convey the intensity with which love, life, and death are felt. Louis – a man turned into a vampire by Lestat de Lioncourt who is a disarming white French man/vampire born in 1760, and who Louis calls "my murderer, my mentor, my lover and my maker" – is both narrator and Nosferatu.

Louis invites us in, while lurking in the shadows – so close, yet also so far away. After the show's finish, his familiar and fervent drawl echoes: "It was a cold winter that year, and Lestat was my coal fire", and "For the first time in my life, I was seen." These are just two of many lines that Louis utters, having never felt "okay" in a maddening world within which he exists as a Black and gay man, and delivering statements to the audience that are as delicious as devastating.

There is a long history of the Gothic being associated with blackness, yet Black people and the Gothic are still quite a rare pairing in pop culture. As Andrew Keahey wrote in an article for The Black Youth Project, "We deserve to see more Black vampires on the screen,"[20] including in the Gothic setting of shows that span different eras. Yet, as is highlighted in the brilliant book, *The Black Guy Dies First: Black Horror Cinema from Fodder to Oscar*, by Robin R. Means Coleman and Mark H. Harris, Black vampires are not new and are part of Black horror history.[21] This includes singer and actor Aaliyah's portrayal of Queen Akasha in *Queen of the Damned* (2002), a loose sequel to *Interview with the Vampire: The Vampire Chronicles* (1994).

Interview with the Vampire (2022–present) brings aspects of Black Gothic horror to the front and centre, while departing from the sexual puritanism that was part of the *Twilight* film saga and other depictions of chaste vampires in the 2000s/2010s. The show does so through Louis and a Black girl called Claudia (evocatively portrayed by Bailey Bass in season 1 and Delainey Hayles in season 2). Louis saved Claudia from a fire when she was 14 years-old, and, upon his request, she is turned into a vampire by Lestat (who previously turned Louis). Claudia's physical appearance doesn't age, but her mind and outlook become that of an adult over time. As the three of them form a dysfunctional domestic dynamic, the sense of sibling-like closeness between Louis and Claudia sparks discord between him and Lestat. The reasons for such disharmony are many, including the jealousy of Lestat, whose insecurities, among other feelings, manifest through his efforts to control Louis.

A current that courses throughout *Interview with the Vampire* is messages about the power of emotions, perceptions, memories, and dreams, in addition to the horrors of numbness and the controlling actions of individuals with the power to sedate others. When witnessing the show's exploration of people (or queer vampires) living life loudly and facing the risks of doing so out in the open, you may be reminded of the challenges faced by those who are oppressed in real life. Undoubtedly, vampires on this show are far from "okay" and are represented as flawed, but they are also represented as boldly refusing to submit to their societal suppression. In turn, such characters hold a mirror up to some of the monstrous actions and attitudes of humans, while also reflecting both the fight against, and freedom from, certain types of repression.

As observed by writers s.e. smith in 2019 and Melanie McFarland in 2022, a rise of media and literature about vampires can be symptomatic of economic downturns and accompanying desires for escapism that offer entertaining outlets for engaging existential ideas about life (and death).[22] Vampire-related pop culture can also respond to, reflect, or reimagine racial, gender, and sexual politics, such as power dynamics that are part of music, movies, and the messages that they express. With that in mind, the next chapter deepens our discussion of portrayals of monsters, narratives of (im)mortality, and the meaningfulness of memories, by focusing on materiality, moons, and myths.

Chapter 3
Feeling Music and Movies: On Materiality, Moons, and Myths

Record Store Day is on the calendar of many music lovers. Created in 2007, in support of vinyl records and independent stores that home them, the annual day includes new releases, exclusive reissued music, and live performances. There have been points throughout history when vinyl sales have waxed and waned, but demand for vinyl has flourished since Record Store Day's creation. For the 16th consecutive year, sales of vinyl records in the UK have increased,[23] resulting in reports that question the reasons behind this uptick. In 2023, US vinyl album sales rose for the 17th consecutive year, but growth was noted as slowing.[24] Despite that change, vinyl made up more than 40% of album sales. That same year, unit-sales of vinyl records rose by 11.7% in the UK, making this the highest level for the UK's vinyl market since 1990.[25] While vinyl sales have increased, record player sales haven't followed an identical pattern.

In 2024, Luminate – a music and entertainment data provider – reported that just 50% of people who purchase vinyl in the US have a record player.[26] So, what drives vinyl sales? Answers might touch on the longer history of collecting and music fandom practices, but the role of *feeling(s)* in this is sometimes overshadowed by the idea that people simply want to "own" music.

Questions about why people without a record player would purchase vinyl often overlook communal experiences of music listening: time spent at the homes of friends, family, and loved ones, or in rare community-centered public spaces, where a record player is ready and waiting. As Jenessa Williams reflects on in "Tracing Music Fandom Practice Through The Internet": "I can, of course, remember a childhood before it [the internet] – buying magazines and CDs, making mixtapes by taping the radio top 40, texting into music TV stations to request my favourite song…"[27] Today, cassettes and CDs continue to be created, such as for Bob Vylan's eclectic *Humble as the Sun* (2024) album, featuring a glowing cover which is part of how the music may be felt.

As is emphasised in the work of Joy White on *Like Lockdown Never Happened: Music and Culture During*

COVID, "Over the last few decades, advances in digital technology have made all forms of popular music more accessible"[28]. In an age when lots of encounters with music are mediated by digital platforms and algorithms, the materiality of music remains meaningful to many people – whether it's how they connect to and through music in physical spaces, or the sensation of sifting through a box of vinyl to find the record(s) your heart yearns for.

Music's materiality is as much about feeling(s) as it's about the machinations of markets. This means that to understand the many different reasons why people are drawn to vinyl records, cassettes, and CDs – beyond the opportunity to hear music or purchase a "collectible" – we need to think about why such music formats and all that they hold touch people. As their shape suggests, vinyl records present people with a form of circularity and wholeness, but they are far from solely being a sound on loop. From the beat of your heart as a vinyl's grooved vibrations reach you, to the sense of anticipation when inching a record out of its sleeve, there are many paired parts to vinyl's physicality and to music's textures – meaning that experiences of vinyl listening are set apart from listening to music through online streaming platforms.

More than Images, Mythologising, and Memorialising

At this point, a pause/paws for thought might be welcomed.

Given the many ways that record players and other material objects related to music have been associated with images of dogs, we want to reflect on these beloved animals, including a terrier-mix dog named Nipper (also known as the RCA Victor dog). Nipper, from Bristol in England, was treated as a posthumous model for a painting in 1898, titled "His Master's Voice" (HMV) by Francis Barraud. That became a well-known visual of the dog and a gramophone, which would go on to be an iconic image used by record companies and associated company brands. Eventually, the image also became part of the logo for HMV Retail Ltd, a British music and entertainment retailer, founded in 1921. Although many people may be familiar with different versions of images of Nipper, significantly fewer people could name the dog. This signals some of the countless ways that dogs and other animals are often treated as more of a source of entertainment or means to an end, than (another) being to be loved and cared for/about[29].

Street sign depicting a dog's silhouette in Paris, June 2024. Photograph by Francesca Sobande

"His Master's Voice" record player at The People's Museum of Limerick, July 2023. Photograph by Francesca Sobande

"A super 1987 set of 4 stamps commemorating
Transport Events. Price: 25p", October 2024.
Photograph by Francesca Sobande

It's not only dogs who've been treated as objectified icons, surrounded by spectacle. Some people have been positioned in similar ways. This includes consumer culture's oppressive (re)presentation of certain famous musicians as iconic. Some musicians welcome their iconicity. Others critique how musicians and their work's messages are destructively reframed when they are just treated as a celebrity and, simply, as a symbol.

The word *icon* stems from Latin via the Greek *eikon*, meaning "likeness, image". Viewing someone as an icon involves an *idea* and *impression* of them, rather than truly knowing or embracing them. For these reasons, assigning someone an iconic status – even fondly – can mean treating them as more of a disembodied image than an individual who feels too.

Both in life and death, many famous musicians and singers have been subjected to objectifying and mythologising portrayals of them, rendered as more of an idea than receiving recognition and respect as a whole person. This includes narratives that gloss over the principles and beliefs expressed through their music. We witnessed this on the day of the death of Irish singer-songwriter Shuhada' Sadaqat, who performed under the name Sinéad O'Connor (1966–2023) but took the name Shuhada' Sadaqat after converting to Islam in 2018.

At the time her death was announced, we were in Castleconnell in the Republic of Ireland. Despite its bereft tone, global media coverage tiptoed around matters that Sadaqat stood for and spoke up about. A plaintive but noticeably partial picture was painted by most outlets. It was a picture that didn't dare mention the impactful lyrics and titles of songs such as "Black Boys on Mopeds" which called out the cruelties of the

Conservative government in Britain and the endemic nature of racism, something that she consistently addressed.

Indeed, some media commentaries mentioned Sadaqat's vocal denouncement of the Catholic church's abuses and the backlash she faced. Yet, few went beyond a brief nod to that, failing to acknowledge the many ways that Sadaqat challenged multiple forms of oppression and injustice. Even fewer media reports referred to Sadaqat by that name, signifying society's focus on iconicity and the mythologising of those deemed "performers" – in this case, a mediated focus on (re)presentations of Sinéad O'Connor's image and ideas of her, rather than embracing both the music of the artist known as O'Connor *and* the entirety of Shuhada' Sadaqat. Relationships between media, mythic iconicity, memorialising, and music are part of many moments and memories of/in life, including, as we now focus on, the movie *The Crow* (1994).

Moons, Memories, and *The Crow*

Eric Draven is a name at the centre of the cinematic world of *The Crow*. This includes the original 1994 film featuring Brandon Lee as Draven, in his tragic last performance before his death due to an accident on set at the age of 28. As Lee said of the crow in the film,

"You could really just look at it as a guide…almost a piece of his [Eric Draven's] own personality who guides him back into his life and reminds him who he was… what happened to him. This is a person who has been pushed right to the limits of his ability to cope with what is going on, and in a sense is quite mad sometimes, in a sense is completely insane…"[30]

A painting of a crow and the surrounding art materials.
July 2024. Painting and photograph
by Francesca Sobande

Out of context, nothing about the name Eric Draven screams metal, but *The Crow* is anything but bland.

Based on the 1989 comic by James O'Barr and which became a comic series, films about *The Crow* deal with the intensity of loss and the infiniteness of love. They follow Draven as he seeks to avenge the brutal assault and murder of him and his love, taking the audience on a journey towards realising, as articulated in the final scene: "It can't rain all the time." Audiences witness that, in Lee's words during his last interview, "There are no rules about how someone who has come back from the dead is going to behave." The equally contemplative closing line of the 1994 film sums up its hopeful feelings: "If the people we love are stolen from us, the way to have them live on is to never stop loving them. Buildings burn…people die…but real love is forever."

There is nothing more metal and *real* than the eternity of love. And perhaps, in some sense, Lee's powerful portrayal of Draven is one of many blueprints for what would become known as the on-screen "softboy/boi" – a man attuned to the depths of emotions, refusing to shy away from the vulnerabilities of love, loss, and their links.

Such sentiments include Lee's poignant words on the brevity and beauty of life, as well as the significance of memories: "Because we do not know when we will die, we get to think of life as an inexhaustable well, and yet everything only happens a certain number of times, and a very small number really...how many more times will you remember a certain afternoon of your childhood...an afternoon that's so deeply a part of your being that you can't even conceive of your life without it?...Perhaps 4 or 5 times more...perhaps not even that...How many more times might you watch the full moon rise? Perhaps, 20, and yet it all seems limitless...". When reflecting on that, sadness might surface, but you might also feel forms of softness that gleam through Lee's moving meditation on memories, moons, and mortality.

There is a languidness and luminosity to *The Crow* (1994), no matter how painful its subject matter is. Even though the visual landscapes of it are mostly monochromatic, with scenes soaked in stirring shadows and framed by stark black silhouettes, the vivid nature of love finds a way to glisten. Relatedly, the metal qualities of the 1994 film *The Crow* have long been emphasised, including as part of commentaries on its electric soundtrack and emotional story. The '94 take on *The Crow* is certainly not the only example of pop culture that melds together metal, moviemaking, and messages of (im)mortality and memorialising. As mentioned earlier, another film which draws heavily on the Gothic and metal is *Queen of the Damned* (2002) – a text that symbolises how the iconicity of Black women is simultaneously engaged and erased as part of the making and marketing of movies, (nu-)metal, and their union.

Consuming *Queen of The Damned* and Black Women

Queen of the Damned (2002) is another media text based on Anne Rice's *Vampire Chronicles* books. The film follows the lore of Lestat de Lioncourt during his time as The Rockstar. Depending on your reference point, Lestat may be mostly associated with Brad Pitt's 1994 *Interview with the Vampire* portrayal, Stuart Townsend's interpretation in *Queen of the Damned*, or the 2022 onwards TV performance of Sam Reid. Playing Lestat with a charisma that makes his every on-screen movement transfixing, Reid's portrayal complicates binary ideas of good and bad, pleasure and pain, masculinity and femininity, life and death.

At the time of writing this, season three of *Interview with the Vampire* is due for release in 2025, with the musical teaser for it showcasing Lestat's Rockstar era. This has led to people questioning how the TV series might connect to or depart from *Queen of the Damned*, which depicted Lestat as seduced by the powerful vampire and "baddie" – a term we'll return to later – Akasha (played by R&B and hip-hop singer and actress Aaliyah, marking the last on-screen role before her tragic death in a plane crash at 22).

Notably, *Queen of the Damned* is soundtracked by nu-metal music (overseen by Jonathan Davis of Korn), which plays a key part in the plot. As a genre that took force near the end of one century and the beginning of another, nu-metal is often synonymous with nostalgia for the 2000s. The genre brings together features of '90s grunge, '80s hair metal, '70s funk, and even, at times, '60s psychedelic sonics, while also being significantly shaped by rap, R&B, and hip-hop across various decades (e.g. Linkin Park's inventive collaboration with Jay-Z for the 2004 album *Collision Course*).

Influenced by it, nu-metal came together years after the development of speed-metal, a genre which music journalist Dele Fadele described as having sprung "from a semi-political do-your-own-thing stance with only riffs as common ground. It still values 'the street', 'the kids' who've been drawn up into a nihilistic vortex and are actually confronted by Bad Brains and their ilk."[31] Writing about the powerhouse impact of Bad Brains in the "Editors' Notes" of *Black Punk Now: Fiction, Non-fiction and Comics*, Chris L. Terry remarks, "Even today, when I talk about Black punk, Bad Brains are the first name that people mention. They deserve it. They are the first and best hardcore punk band."[32] Among the many people who Bad Brains have impacted is Santigold – someone familiar with having their work miscategorised and overlooked due to assumptions about blackness and music. During a 2022 NPR Music's Tiny Desk Concert Santigold fondly spoke about punk being at her roots as a performer, reminiscing about playing with Bad Brains in Washington D.C. in the earlier days.[33]

By the time that nu-metal and adjacent genres rose, including bands such as Body Count (fronted by rapper and actor Ice-T), the creative influence of Bad Brains was apparent across many planes of music, even if this is often omitted from music history. Arguably, scarce musicians, bands, and artists have mustered up such politically powerful work as Bad Brains (their self-titled album cover which features a lightning bolt striking D.C.'s Capitol Building remains as resonant as ever), instead, seemingly opting for more of a style over substance or sound without soul approach. Music should stand for something.

That said, for all its faults, nu-metal has heart. It reflects the crises and connectedness presented by life's finiteness – think Papa Roach's "Between Angels and Insects" (2000). This makes it a fitting soundtrack to the *Queen of the Damned*, a film that foregrounds vampires and nu-metal while also featuring an R&B and hip-hop icon. In some ways, this pairing of nu-metal and Aaliyah's bold presence symbolises that blackness and Black music is integral to the genre. Although Aaliyah doesn't sing in the film, she invokes the reality that, far from what is sometimes implied, R&B and hip-hop are a distinct part of (nu-)metal, not disconnected from or peripheral to it. Acknowledging this doesn't take away from the fact that these are genres that have their own identities and idiosyncrasies. Rather, recognising connections between R&B, hip-hop, and nu-metal can create a more meaningful understanding of each, their history, and the racial and gender politics of music and its fluctuating categorisation.

Queen of the Damned is part of media and music that tells us something about nu-metal and its (de)fanged nature – we argue, its twinned embrace and disavowal of Black women, as represented by the ways that Akasha animates this nu-metal film while, ultimately, being annihilated by it. Among *Queen of the Damned's* issues are what seem to be vapid messages about deferential and assimilationist approaches to multiculturalism, with vampires – particularly fronted by Akasha – seeming like collective proxies for real people of colour, who are positioned as needing to integrate into the "human" world (or else...). Other irksome aspects of the film include its cloying closing shot in London, lingering in the blurred shadows of "cool Britannia" messaging and the abrupt overthrow of the on-screen Black villain. There's much more to *Queen of the Damned* than that, but when (re)watching the film and reading critiques of Akasha's character, it's clear how *Queen of the Damned* and its nu-metal image benefits from blackness (specifically, *Black women*) while also unceremoniously scorning it.

Akasha is depicted as seeking retribution for the treatment of vampires by humans, rather than wanting to blend into their "moral" world. Not long after a clichéd rose-petals in the bath and blurred bedroom scene (soundtracked by Deftones), Akasha is destroyed by several vampires who view her as vengeful and destructive. When accounting for the fact that Akasha is the only prominent Black character in the film, and a Black woman at that, we can't help but think about parallels between the positioning and punishing of her, and that of real Black women who are impacted by what writer, scholar, and activist Moya Bailey termed "misogynoir"[34] – capturing the interconnected force of anti-Black racism, sexism, and misogyny.[35]

Given the film's nu-metal qualities, combined with its use of visual allusions to the ambiguous non-West, and the exoticisation of Akasha, *Queen of the Damned* depicts how nu-metal takes up *and* turns away from Black women. Here, a Black woman is both salient and treated as a torment – it's Akasha's audacious on-screen presence which, to draw on bell hooks' work on "Eating the Other,"[36] adds "flavour" to the film, before Akasha is literally consumed by other (white) vampires. So, Akasha's character and the end she meets is analogous with some of the experiences of Black women in nu-metal, adjacent genres/subcultures, and in a society where many people feel entitled to look at, touch, and consume Black women in objectifying and oppressive ways.

Megan Thee Stallion, "Alt" Music, and Baddiecore

Rightly praised for her lyrical dynamism, powerful performances and rapping and musical prowess, Megan Thee Stallion is an artist who defies stale ideas about the boundaries of music categories. Her song "Cobra", which at the time of writing this has been viewed more than 25 million times on YouTube, foregrounds aesthetics and atmospheres associated with snakes and regeneration. The song and music video for it opens with a line about a snake shedding its skin, featuring footage of Megan Thee Stallion's mouth uttering that from a black background – momentarily rendering her as being much more heard than simply seen.

The opening shot of the "Cobra" music video might also be thought of as calling back to footage of the unnamed Black woman radio DJ in the 1979 film *The Warriors*, a character who takes shape through her unique voice and close-up footage of her mouth. As the person who runs a radio programme and that the street gangs in *The Warriors* tune into, the radio DJ is omniscient throughout the film – somehow an authoritative yet unknowable person – evading hypervisibility while also being far from invisible. In that sense, both the character of the radio DJ and the footage of Megan Thee Stallion early in the "Cobra" music video are impactfully opaque (re)presentations of Black women – breaking free of the media's fixation on looking at *but not* listening to them.

"Cobra (Rock Remix)", featuring the heavy metal band Spiritbox, catalysed a chorus of online comments about Megan Thee Stallion, metal music, and the view that, in the words of *MusicWeek*: "No one saw that coming."[37] While some expressed surprise at the remix and called into question the potential for it to be labelled metal – even suggesting that Spiritbox had somehow sold out by collaborating on the track, others pointed out that the work of Megan Thee Stallion has long had a closeness to iterations of "alternative" ("alt") rock. By October 2024, both acts had collaborated again on the track "TYG".

Rock's influence and infusing in "Cobra" is evident in the original version, and in the overall roster of music by Megan Thee Stallion, not just in the remix with Spiritbox. Despite that, and consistent with how the Rock qualities of Black music and musicians are constantly questioned, her work's connections to alternative music are often flouted – echoing the well-established ways that "altness" is generally reimagined as white, and, mostly, male. Here, drawing on the work of Maureen Mahon on *Black Diamond Queens: African American Women and Rock and Roll* serves as a reminder of the reality that "[s]ince the 1950s, when they were among the rhythm and blues artists who created the music that took the name *rock and roll*, African American women have made pivotal contributions to the form as it underwent decades of stylistic and cultural changes. Stories of their involvement in rock and roll, however, have been marginal to the dominant narrative, and, like Santi White [Santigold], they have been pressed into genres deemed appropriate for African American women or not talked about at all."[38]

One of numerous examples of media and reporting coverage of Megan Thee Stallion, which trivialises her interest in and association with alt rock, focusing more on her physical appearance, is a *Loudwire* piece titled "Megan Thee Stallion Vamps to Static-X Song On Instagram, Band + Fans React."[39] Commenting on a viral post by her, the article opens with the statement: "Megan Thee Stallion turned heads on Monday when she showed off her assets in a suggestive video on Instagram that shows her vamping to the Static-X song 'Cold'." Referred to as a "spicy clip" that "elicited a response from Static-X and several Rock and Metal fans,"[40] the post by Megan Thee Stallion (described as a "hip hop artist and celebrity spokesperson") was treated with a fascination that seems steeped in the idea that there's something remarkable about a Black woman in hip-hop enjoying metal.

As mentioned in the *Loudwire* piece, "The Static-X song 'Cold' appears in its original form on the band's second album, *Machine* (2001). It also appears in a different version on the *Queen of the Damned* soundtrack (2002)." With this in mind, it's useful to reflect on connections between Megan Thee Stallion's music, the *Vampire Chronicles*, and metal/alt rock.

Beyond the Static-X song connection, the world of the *Vampire Chronicles* was recently positioned in proximity to Megan Thee Stallion through social media. This was following her response to a September 2024 X post that asked: "Have you seen Interview with the Vampire series on Netflix?? #HOTGIRLVMAS", with "No but thee hotties [the affectionate name for her fans] seem to like it so I might need to tune in lol #HOTGIRLVMAS."[41] That exchange is consistent with what Jenessa Williams points out about internet music fan practices from the 2010s onwards, "…a boom in musical social media use continued. Fan-led taste-making was becoming more prominent in the generation of 'viral' hits, but so was artist engagement, able to reply to fan messages or distribute blog posts with more ease and creativity than previously possible."[42]

Since the posts about *Interview with the Vampire* between Megan Thee Stallion and fans, there have been calls for her to take on the role of Akasha in the third season. Such calls nod to the presence of Black women in hip-hop[43], specifically in the on-screen *Vampire Chronicles* world and in alt rock spheres: that is, Aaliyah as the "baddie" in *Queen of the Damned*, and Megan Thee Stallion's rock associations.

On the topic of "baddies", recent iterations of metal music have led to the tongue-in-cheek sub-genre descriptor "baddiecore", since Stray from the Path's drummer Craig Reynolds posted: "how do sub genre names stick? like djent and nu metal etc? because i got one that i call bands like sleep token, bad omens and spiritbox. baddiecore. metalcore with enough pop music crossover and sex appeal that normie hot people like it. i hate it so much i love it."[44] Commentaries on "baddiecore" sometimes focus on the sexualisation of songs and those who are behind them, but the label is often used in response to metalcore which calls back to the dulcet tones and demure-yet-dramatic demeanour of R&B and hip-hop, including what's sometimes termed "bedroom" music, and smooth sounds associated with "yacht rock."[45]

In the words of legendary record producer and composer Quincy Jones, in *Quincy* (2018) – a documentary about his life, "In order for music to grow, the critics must stop categorising and let the musicians get involved in all different facets of music. We will die if we get stuck in one area of music." Also, as Maureen Mahon affirms in *Black Diamond Queens: African American Women and Rock and Roll*, "Genre categories simplify things for music business professionals, whether at record labels, music venues, or media outlets; they help identify an artist's potential audience and determine how to promote their music. As such, genre labels have a powerful effect on the shape and direction of an artist's career."[46] Nowadays though, certain genre and sub-genre terms, such as "baddiecore", are the outcome of digital discourse which differs to top-down and traditional industry processes of establishing genre categories.

Although it's not usually acknowledged amid commentaries concerning baddiecore, the term "baddie" (usually, a derivative of "bad bitch") is strongly connected to Black American cultural expressions. It is especially used in reference to Black women who are perceived as being self-possessed. This connection is apparent when recalling that, as heavy metal journalist and scholar Laina Dawes notes, "Especially for black women, who are often told from an early age that we have to be more aware of how others perceive us, how we appear in society is often more important than asserting our individuality."[47] This means that the ability to embody a sense of self-governance – being a "baddie"– is hard fought for by Black women – including, but not limited to, Black women sex workers, who face societal projections of their presumed strength, subjugation, and sensualities.

When accounting for this, and that "baddiecore" is mainly used to describe predominantly white and/or male bands, it makes the term seem like yet another that may (inadvertently) gloss over the racial, sexual, and gender politics of metal/alt rock. Specifically, much like what Akasha in *Queen of the Damned* seems to symbolise, certain framings of "baddiecore" signal how Black culture and creativity (*especially that of Black women*) is both hyper-visible and invisible in metal. What is baddiecore *without baddies*? Current discussions, debates, and digital content about "baddiecore" also reflect how social media activity influences ideas about words, their meaning, and uptake. Mindful of that, we turn our attention to so-called "internet speak".

Chapter 4
Something is Off/Online: On Social Media Spectacle and Digital Life

For the Gram
Sending Me
Chronically Online
LMR (like my recent)
Why did you block me?

Everything is In Real Life (IRL)

The term "internet speak" is commonly used to refer to phrases that are well-known online. Many of such expressions originate from the vernaculars, linguistic styles, and oral histories of structurally oppressed people, such as Black and LGBTQIA+ communities. Social media's fixation on condensing means that the details of many matters are often lost in people's pursuit of posting something pithy and popular. We witness the reduction and reframing of who and where expressions stem from, when hashtags and topics discussed online are merely positioned as the by-product of the internet.

Social media's influence on uses and interpretations of words includes the impact of how certain subjects and connected comments are censored there. People find ways to still discuss sensitive topics that are stifled on such sites, including by using proxy terms to work around the suppression of associated words. In this contentious context, catch-all terms such as "un-alived" have been used instead of "suicide" and "murder".

Although the reasoning behind some people's use of these proxy terms relates to an effort to evade censorship of speech on social media, some of these expressions (e.g. "un-alived") are also uttered offline. In 2024 this was highlighted by online media responses to an exhibition at Seattle's Museum of Pop Culture, where a placard about frontman of Nirvana, Kurt Cobain, used the words "un-alived himself" to refer to Cobain's death by suicide at 27.[48]

The exhibition also included a placard briefly explaining the digital culture from which the term "un-alived" has sprouted, alluding to different views of its (un)helpfulness. Then again, as pointed out by critiques, use of "un-alive(d)" – especially beyond online spaces where the word "suicide" might be suppressed – can trivialise people's deaths and infantilise those who are being spoken to about them. The combination of that can be insensitive narratives that close off the space to truly acknowledge the severity of what has happened and how people are impacted by that. In turn, there may be diminished potential for people to connect with related forms of help.

Is There Anybody Out There?

Connecting with others involves more than just bearing witness, such as by going beyond voyeuristically looking at social media posts. Still, due to the power of the internet and digital technology, it can play a pivotal role in how people cultivate and contribute to forms of support that transcend borders – be they the borders of digital screens or the borders of physical places and spaces. In addition to being somewhere that people connect, social media sites can and do produce profit.

The overt presence of advertising, marketing, and commerce in social media has been especially clear since the 2010s. From that point onwards, many brands have used social media in ways that sustain their communications and business strategy. As the (imagined) lines between online communities, countercultures, and consumer culture began to disintegrate with the movements of the third millennium, the space to share and connect with other people online seemed to explode *and* implode.

More and more social media sites, platforms, and apps appeared (Instagram, Snapchat, TikTok), while others disappeared or ceased to remain relevant (Bebo, MySpace, Vine). People continued to disclose, document, and depict moments and musings to audiences out (t)here. But there was decreasing scope to do so in ways that stay within the relatively unobserved digital homes of fandom communities and subcultures. The prospect of going (semi)viral, becoming internet famous, and accruing momentary notoriety, or a longer lasting microcelebrity status, started to seem within reach for more people. As a result, there began to be more public commentary about the idea of online fame, and, eventually, terms such as "content creator" cropped up.

Between brands' attempts to humanise their image and the powerful impact of artificial intelligence (AI), social media is now a crowded space where it can be difficult to determine who is behind a post – *is there anybody out there?* Still, as editor and writer Ione Gamble notes in *Poor Little Sick Girls*, "With the internet and social media allowing marginalised people total autonomy over their stories – perhaps for the first time in modern history – our narratives have never been easier to disseminate across the world."[49] Conversely, as Gamble also points out, "While collective action grouped my peers and me together as I came of age, individual recognition is now the driving motivation for many currently operating online."

Social media's emphasis on attention-grabbing aesthetics, searchable soundbites, censoring, and categorising posts contributes to the mainstreaming of discussions and depictions that were once peripheral to consumer culture. In other words, does the saturation of social media and the ascent of AI mark the death of subcultures? Can countercultures remain so within the confines of online sites, platforms, and apps? The intense spectacle and surveillance systems surrounding social media and AI can mean an absence of space for true subversiveness. But we live in a world where, in many situations, access to digital technology and the internet is a matter of life or death. So, we must still work to tackle the pervasive power regimes that position and pathologise oppressed people (online and offline) as nothing more than disturbances and disturbed.

(Don't) Touch Me I'm (not) Sick

During the ongoing COVID-19 pandemic, many nations introduced contact tracing apps to determine whether an individual or an area posed a risk of infection and to permit or deny people the right to leave their homes or enter a particular area. Many of these apps were designed by big tech companies – for example, Apple and Google – in collaboration with state authorities, providing a clear example of how the data that is gathered and processed by companies can be used by governments for surveillance of the population. Whilst social media encourages users to share, share, share everything from selfies and significant life moments to your approximate location, emphasis is put on you being in control of what information is shared and any data sharing undertaken by companies is done to provide a personalised service to you, the user.

For those navigating borders, national and supranational authorities, the capturing and sharing of biometric data – which includes fingerprints, facial images, and iris scans – is non-negotiable and promoted as a solution to potential (perceived) security threats. In a shift to a fully digital immigration system, the UK's Home Office has been gradually replacing physical immigration documents with an eVisa, claiming it will be quicker and easier for immigration status to be proved at the UK border, and for the status to be shared with third parties like employers and landlords. In addition, it will also record biometric details and the conditions of, permission, to enter or stay in the UK. Only once an individual has *become* a British citizen will their biometric data be deleted and, given the lengthy and convoluted process of applying for citizenship, biometric data can be held for many years. Biometrics are also taken from people who the UK deems to be in the country 'unlawfully', including those who are seeking asylum, have been detained under the Immigration Acts and those subject to being deported from the UK. This includes children. Such information can be kept for an indeterminable time.

As migrants, the full complexity and wholeness of personhood is reduced to data within systems, namelessness and perceived neediness by the society they hope to become part of. To be considered worthy of care and feeling can only be achieved through narratives of destitution – here and there – not the horrors of imperialism and the migrant routes made by them. The reality that many Western societies are built by and rely on extraction and exploitation of countries rich in resources to sustain a minority is erased. Instead, an illusion is manufactured. Despite quality of conditions and resources in many Western countries being in decline for some time, they are made to appear desirable to 'the Other'. People are encouraged to see resources as being in short supply and their needs in direct competition, enabling further alienation and criticism of the crisis of care to be side-stepped.

In lockdown periods of the COVID-19 pandemic, life, death, living and dying were played out on and offline. Messages scrawled on pavements, drawn on windows and stuck to shuttered shopfronts offered alternative forms of communication to those able to get outside and who, perhaps, weren't online. During this period, the UK was one of several countries whose acknowledgement of the extreme working conditions faced by care and health workers became a nationwide weekly event. On Thursday evenings, at doorways and from balconies, people clapped their appreciation for the NHS, supported by social media hashtags such as #ClapForOurCarers and #ThankYouNHS. Little was said of decades long underfunding of the NHS and the sub-inflationary pay rises faced by its workers since 2008[50] nor of the discomfort felt by the implied sense of duty and obligation to publicly make visible support for healthcare workers. Experiences of other key workers, including those who weren't labelled as such, but who were undertaking (often unpaid) work like helping, cooking, and shopping – crucial to sustaining life – was overlooked and underappreciated.

The Workers' Stories Project goes some way to addressing this by archiving and publishing the stories of workers such as supermarket staff, lorry drivers and administrators from across Scotland who lived and worked through the pandemic.[51] In this project and during recent strike actions, postal workers reflected on never-ending deliveries and the physical demands of the increase in workloads; being unable to access a toilet whilst on shift;

worries of catching or passing on the virus to customers and colleagues, and the huge responsibility of quite often being the only form of human contact for customers isolating at home.

Portrayals of the 'new normal' on social media appeared to depict an understanding of who we *could* be, if liberated from work and jobs. Slowing down manifested in photographs and videos of making meals, homebrews, baking, exercising, knitting, 'new' pets and babies, gardening/tending to plants, and screen-shots of seemingly endless family/friend online quizzes. Such posts warped realities of life under restrictions and attempted to reinforce pre-pandemic norms in the abnormal. It remained important to keep producing, to not slack and perhaps even, turn the hobby into a side hustle/longer term project when 'things went back to normal'. This isn't to say that the pandemic wasn't experienced in the freeing ways (for some people) which some of this content showed, but life and the process of change is messy, and we know much of #PandemicLife was confusing and ugly. Dead or dying plants should be shown, not only the ones which survived/thrived.

Claustrophobic and exhausting grief and guilt, acute loneliness, bone-wearying working conditions, an inability to make sense of mass loss of life and the world that was unfolding, excessive consumption of goods which brought no satisfaction, blurring of work/private/

public life boundaries, intense surveillance, and exposure of living arrangements (perhaps forced) were seldom brought into the fore.

Yet, it is also *some* of these things which are still with us, long after the lifting of restrictions.

A teddy bear sitting beside the road. March 2024.
Photograph by layla-roxanne hill

Pausing, Processing ≠ Progress

In times where crisis is the 'new normal', we have found ourselves trapped between desire for liberation, and fear that any disruption to the everyday could unravel the fragile semblance of normalcy. In trying to pause and process, we are often engaging in further forms of performativity and progress. Even rest feels like it needs to be productive.

Being mindful and the practicing of mindfulness – to be fully present and aware of where we are and what we're doing, is often facilitated via social media and personal wellness tracking apps. Tools like meditation and journaling apps are marketed as aids for finding calm and peace, yet many have built-in metrics and prompts that turn them into a scheduled and structured activity with measurable achievements. Other wellness and learning apps encourage daily streaks, shifting the focus to consistency and not about creating a free space to explore the practice in its fullness – and make mistakes whilst doing so.

If a meditative and healing practice like listening to music is undertaken via apps such as Spotify, instead of being able to enjoy remembering and *feeling* the familiar, the listener is often encouraged to discover the next thing they *might* 'like'. Unless a Spotify user enters into a 'Private Session', what might be thought of as a personal and private moment is actually being shared much more publicly and widely with followers of that Spotify profile (yes, it's likely your current/former lover, colleague or friend knows you are listening to *that* song on repeat in the dead of the night). And even in a Private Session, Spotify is always listening, watching and profiting from your data.

Algorithms work to offer suggestions, find 'new' music and create 'new' playlists based on previous listening behaviour. A human listener could be directed towards seemingly meaningful music and listen to popular tracks, believing the amount of plays a song has, has been created by people just like them, in a shared (but mostly anonymous) listening experience. However, it's become known that Spotify has been flooded by artificial streaming (bot accounts 'listening' to songs to boost streaming numbers) and music by artists who don't exist, in the form of AI which has been trained on 'real' artists. The more songs which are 'listened' to by bots – particularly those made by AI – the more it serves to undermine the music industry. Royalties are paid to the AI musicians and (usually) not to smaller real artists already pushed into joining big streaming platforms to try to make royalties from their work. Despite facing criticism regarding the harm AI is already causing to the industry and Spotify CEO Daniel EK admitting that AI's progress is "really cool and scary", he refuses to ban it from the platform.

That's not to say that every song ever made is done so with the depth of desire and feelings it may imply or project, as the many love songs – which are seldom about self-love – we've come to know (and forget) demonstrate. As an industry – particularly in the West – which is wholly part of a capitalist system (not to suggest that all music here is part of markets), this would be impossible. But when songs and listens are stripped of anything beyond being bought and created purely for profit, this changes the relationship we have to music and its makers, as well as its potential for community and healing. It can erode and further distance the connections between creator, performer, listener, artist and fan.

Large scale – and often high-cost – concerts in venues such as The Philippine Arena in Bocaue, Philippines (capacity, 55,000), Co-op Live in Manchester, England (20,000 – 23,500) and Sphere in Las Vegas, USA (18,000 – 20,000) which adopt the gladiatorial feel of Roman amphitheaters, further risks alienating listeners and fans from the experience of *feeling* music. The performer is far away from the audience and may be unable to see or sense disappointment, joy, entrancement, indifference or even relief on the faces of fans – except perhaps on the faces of those who have paid significantly more to be in closer proximity to the artist. Pyrotechnics, gymnastics, intricate costumes and transitions, big lights and big sounds become the show, as does being in the presence of others who can afford tickets. Wanting (or even needing) to see a favoured artist live – to experience closeness with them, the music and fellow fans is very different from going as a status indictor, to prove ability to afford. This experience is far removed from the perceived intimacy of being online with an artist: following, commenting and liking in their everyday – and maybe even receiving acknowledgement of your fandom.

In the podcast *101 Part Time Jobs,*[52] Bob Vylan reflects on venues creating distance between musicians and fans. They say "We made our bones playing independent music venues, that's how we came up… our first show was in the back of a pub. On Friday, we did two shows, we did the bigger show, then did Fighting Cocks the same night… 150 cap… Probably the biggest show they will have there this year and everybody is excited… the venue is excited and we are excited because we get to go and play these small venues again where there is no barrier which is something that we love…When you do a Kentish Town Forum, it's great… But there is a distance between us and the crowd and you get used to it, but it's not how we started... We do Fighting Cocks, there is no barrier and people are pushed onto the stage… It's two different shows… Fighting Cocks, it's a great night for everybody."

At their 2024 gig at Cardiff's Student Union, Bob Vylan thanked The Moon (a different venue in the city, with a capacity of around 140) for welcoming them during their earlier days: "This city holds a very, very special place in our heart…one of our first shows out of England was here…it was in a beautiful venue called The

Moon". A few weeks after that (in November 2024), The Moon announced their closure due to many structural factors, such as the impact of the cost-of-living crisis and financial pressures shaped by the effects of the pandemic, as well as business rates and taxes that hit grassroots venues hard.[53] As acknowledged in a feature in *Clash,* The Moon was a "key alt venue" in Cardiff that embraced a sense of openness and eclectic spirit, as indicated by the many different types of music and gatherings that it supported.[54]

Storytelling through music is not only part of our history, legacies, struggle and futures, music is a source of joy. The role of truly grassroots venues in seeding and showcasing such storytelling is significant, and much needs to be done to ensure they're celebrated and sustained. This includes needing to ensure that those who do this important work are properly financially supported, and not just during times of crisis.

Think of clubs, schools and dancehalls, front rooms or ballrooms, kitchens, showers, gigs, moshpits, the beach or even on the street – arguably, there isn't enough of this – where you've sang, screamed, swayed, headbanged, sweated, alone or beside someone during a banging Bhangra or Afrobeat, doing Thriller, Jerusalema, the Slosh or the Casper Slide Part Two. Music has kept us going, through times of resistance and redemption, and keeps us connected to those of us who are no longer physically present. Barriers melt away.

More analog ways of listening to music – on vinyl, CD or cassette – can offer time to know and (re)familiarise yourself with the wholeness of music. The very process of picking up, turning over, removing sleeves or cases (*very* carefully in the case of sandpaper covered vinyl album, *The Return of the Durutti Column*), opening and closing a deck or drawer, and placing a needle on a vinyl, becomes a tactile ritual – a multi-sensory embodied experience, (re)connecting the listener to *being* with music. Artwork, lyrics, credits and thank yous which can be overlooked in the world of continuous streaming and never-ending playlists become known.

Sharing music and making playlists isn't new, though how it continued to change over the decades is. Long before mainstream access to the internet brought filesharing, down/uploading and streaming services to many (but not all), making cassette mixtapes was one of the first ways for DJs, musicians, and fans to communicate news from and to the underground – bringing talent and subculture to the surface.

The cassette mixtape has its origins in 1970s hip-hop culture, when mixes from block (street) parties were recorded onto cassette and distributed. Block parties were a place where people could come together and express themselves through music and dance for hours, and mixtapes were a physical piece of those parties which DJs would give away or sell.[55] Launched in the

UK in November 1983, it's likely the *Now That's What I Call Music*[56] compilation series was influenced by the commercial success of the initially grassroots hip-hop mixtape and sought to capitalise on this by making a mixtape featuring the 30 UK hit singles – appealing to a much broader audience.

Mixtapes also offered an opportunity for listeners and fans to express and share their own tastes and talents through a specific mix. Hours could be spent, listening to the radio, waiting to (illegally) hit record when the track needed for that mix was finally caught. It took time, patience and care. From carefully writing out the track listing, artist, label, year to maybe sharing notes or a doodle reflecting feelings about the mixtape – or who it was for – beyond the track listing. Musician Daniel Johnston was known for his individually hand-made and often reused cassette tapes, adorned with drawings which he gave to friends and strangers.

Now, many established musicians are releasing and selling mixtapes produced in studio quality – usually for promotion and marketing purposes – blurring the lines between a studio album and the humble mixtape. However, mixtapes continue to play an essential role for up-and-coming artists, and oftentimes on sites such as Bandcamp, the cassette options are sold out. The trend of making mixtapes doesn't appear to have come around just yet, with the option to buy personalised "one of a kind" and "nostalgic" mixtapes being offered from various online outlets. This may be due in part to the fact that cassettes and the playing/recording equipment required are not readily available to access or purchase.

There does currently exist cassette clubs and monthly tape subscriptions, who, "Preserve and nurture cassette culture... and celebrate the essence of physical music and keep the spirit of cassettes alive, connecting a community of like-minded Cassette Culture Connoisseurs."[57] Perhaps as recently seen with photography using camera film, and the ability to work digitally and physically, combined with a growing desire to experience music beyond streaming – to *feel* music – there could be a return to tape. After all, working with cassette necessitates pausing, rewinding and stopping.

A screen which reads "No signal".
Edinburgh 2024. Photograph by layla-roxanne hill

#PositiveVibesOnly

Social media is filled with therapeutic language such as "boundaries" "processing" and "self-care" which are important concepts for people to know and learn about. However, as we touched on earlier, they're often adopted as trends to copy, routines to follow or tasks to complete, and, when used this way, these genuine liberatory practices can lose their depth and meaning. Many skincare and beauty rituals are reframed as a self-care practice, despite many of the products being unethical, unaffordable to most or the routine itself being unrealistic.

As Kate Lindsay writes in *Who's Afraid of These Gen Alpha Queens?*[58] "Every time I open my TikTok For You Page, I see a creator who strikes fear into my heart. She has blonde hair and wears silk pajamas. Her get-ready-with-me routine is more than 10 steps long and includes a serum that retails for $87. She's better than me, and she knows it – and based on her videos, I'm sure she'd tell me to my face. She is 13." Pressure to perform and document self-care becomes part of productivity culture, where people may start feeling that they are 'failing' at self-care, particularly if they don't have the right product to undertake self-care or relax in ways which are filtered through apps such as Instagram and TikTok.

In a context where misogyny, ageism, sexism, ableism, classism, racism, transphobia and body shaming is able to thrive and everyday incidences of these go mostly unchecked but not unfelt, bell hooks offers much to think about on if it is possible to self-care in such conditions, "When we evoke a sense of home as a place where we can renew ourselves, where we can know love and the sweet communion of shared spirit, I think it's important for us to remember that this location of well-being cannot exist in a context of sexist domination."[59]

The 'clean girl' aesthetic is a high maintenance minimalistic, polished 'off-duty model look', aligned with a lifestyle focused on self-care, wellness and a neutral muted palette. Though many aspects of the aesthetics' roots can be found in Black, brown and Latinx histories, notably the wearing of hoop earrings and having barely there make-up – due in part to mainstream make-up brands offering little variety in skin tone. Clean girl is more commonly associated with young white women, celebrities such as Hailey Bieber, Ashley Tisdale (and their accompanying minimalist products), and the barely-there make-up/skincare range by Glossier.[60] Despite receiving challenges from various 'summer and/or girl' microtrend identities, including the 'mob wife', clean girl and its close cousin 'very demure, very mindful'[61] continues to dominate social media.

'hot girl summer' brought to life in 2021 by Megan Thee Stallion fans (aka Hotties), inspired by her 2019 song of the same name,[62] has six pages of community definitions on Urban Dictionary. Described by Megan as "basically just about women – and men – just being unapologetically them, just having a good-ass time", interpretations of hot girl summer vary. Some people just wanted their first summer after the lifting of COVID-19 restrictions to be the best they'd ever had. To others, it was an invitation for women to behave 'badly'.

It could be possible that Megan's Hotties wanted to support her through the death of her mother and grandmother in 2019 and invite her to be unapologetically herself in her grief, something addressed in the 2024 documentary film *Megan Thee Stallion: In Her Words*. Returning to the public eye in 2022 with new album *Traumazine*, Megan stated: "My alter egos have been people that I had to be at those times to be like my armor, like my shield. I had to be Hot-Girl Meg at that time. I love this album because I feel like it's just me talking. It's just Megan. It's not me having to be anybody else."[63] Drawing from a line from her song *Anxiety*, in 2022 Megan also launched *Bad Bitches Have Bad Days Too*,[64] an online archive of mental health care resources for Black and LGBTQIA+ people. Upon launching the site, Megan released a statement saying; "Hotties! You know how much mental wellness means to me, so I created a hub with resources that can help when you might need a hand." Megan has spoken openly about accessing therapy, and the *Bad Bitches Have Bad Days*

Too website contains links to several free therapy organizations, crisis hotlines, and resources specifically for LGBTQIA+ people of color and Black men and women.

'feral girl summer' followed in 2022, along with 'rat girl summer' of 2023, both offering an extension of the freeness suggested by hot girl summer, in addition to a wildness in response to the controlled and meticulous clean girl. In 2024, the biggest challenger to clean girl was 'brat summer' taken from singer Charli xcx's album, *brat*, which also became the Collins Dictionary 2024 word of the year. The term is defined by Collins as an adjective "characterized by a confident, independent, and hedonistic attitude.[65]"

With its cursory nod to grunge and '90s/early '00s aesthetics which are currently in vogue, brat summer appears to have broken beyond the social media-based marketing. In celebration of *brat*, the London Eye was lit up in neon green – the colour associated with the album – and for elections in both the UK and US, the colour scheme was used in political campaigns. Near the end of autumn 2024, graffiti appeared in several locations in a nearby park reading *rip brat*. The artist needn't have worried. A remix album, *Brat And It's Completely Different But Also Still Brat*, appeared four months after. Less poppy than the og *brat* and featuring more sounds and collaborators (who according to music journalist Cat Zhang has too many men who are *Not Brat*)[66] which will also be familiar to elder millennials, *brat* will likely live on (and offline).

Writing in an Instagram post announcing the release of *brat*, Charli xcx tags and gives thanks to people who, "even when I'm being an absolute nightmare you still stand by me and make me feel comfortable to be myself… and at the end of the day, that's exactly what brat is all about: me, my flaws, my fuck ups, my ego all rolled into one.[67]" Scrolling through both Megan Thee Stallion and Charli xcx's Instagram accounts, it certainly looks like they are living unapologetically as themselves. But, with many posts appearing beautiful, effortless yet posed, clean girl aesthetic sometimes permeates. There may be no room for ugly, but as Ismatu Gwendolyn writes, there is no safety in being beautiful.[68]

"RIP brat." spray painted onto a plinth in a Glasgow park, September 2024. Photograph by layla-roxanne hill

How can musicians known for having perfectly crafted alter-egos, frequent changes of appearance and/or sound – often to suit record labels and their shareholders – promote being themselves? (Then again, many people's everyday lives involve some level of performance and an altering of their image.) It seems that fans are not only promoting the artist and their music, but also any idea and/or aesthetic which is likely to accompany a release. Who is to tell if this is coming from the artists themselves or PR and marketing staff who understand the value of organic social media promotion.

Social media and the microtrend aesthetics created by its users can be a community-building tool, allowing people to connect with others who share similar identities and interests. This has been particularly true of people who have struggled to see themselves represented in traditional or mainstream media, such as for those living in smaller towns or rural settings. However, even with the world's always on and connectedness, we live in increasingly lonely and alienating times. People sought community long before social media and are still looking for that sense of belonging and home. This can be seen from the ever-changing adoption of identities – even if often created by brands – to the interchangeable political messages in people's windows. But communities cannot be built around consumption and consumerism – no matter how much the idea of community is marketed.

To return to bell hooks, in a community, a person needs to share a commitment to the well-being of the relational life which unites them, not focus on promoting their individual identity within the community. Or indeed promoting a product, be that a person or aesthetic.

Conclusion
Windows, Wanders/ Wonders, and (Wild)flowers

I Still Remember

The title of a 2007 Bloc Party song and three words that capture so many emotions, and experiences – longing, lingering, love, and more. *Look, Don't Touch* was penned from feelings of I/we still remember, including an accompanying sense of softness and sharpness, as well as slowness and speed.

Memory can be a fickle thing. It can also be much more powerful and permanent than some people care or are able to consider, and much more enduring and expansive than "scientific research" could ever "evidence". The heart remembers.[69]

From our hearts, we wrote through a whirling vortex of decisions, dreams, disturbances, (dis)embodiments, desires, disruptions, and daily life. You could say that our book is the outcome of days, months, and years spent with different people, animals, plants, atmospheres, and planetary alignments (Mercury's in retrograde right now, yet again). Put simply: *everything's connected* and *everything's messy.*

Open Windows

Connectedness continues to present possibilities – open windows to unknowns and alternatives that may bring better days.

There is nothing quite like feeling the breeze through an open window during a heatwave or on a heavy and hemmed in day: the moment the air reaches you, tickling the nape of your neck with the arrival of the outside. A nearness to otherwise and elsewhere from wherever you are planted or uprooted from. An open window can feel like an invitation to (re)connect with your surroundings and yourself. It's a beacon of hope during a stifling closedness. It can involve forms of holding, releasing, and the tingle of touch – the sensation of connection to what lies beyond the window's frame, and the feeling of movement or being moved. It's both stirring and stilling: "What light through yonder window breaks?"[70] "You are the light. It's not on you, it's in you."[71]

Windows can create space – even if small – to feel relief from forms of containment. Open windows can be part of how you let someone or something in or let someone or something out. They can contribute to how we feel close or far away. There's a reason why windowless rooms are used as part of the brutalities of incarceration and torture, denying people connection to what lies beyond confined solitary spaces.

The saying "window to the soul" conveys that windows are associated with profound insights, such as truly knowing someone and what makes their heart sing or beat faster. This may sound like a romantic view of windows and life, but who said romance is dead? Think, beckoning calls from the street by a lover to another, the remnants of sweetheart messages written on misted panes of glass, and the poetic sight, sound, or smell of the day morphing into a moonlit midnight sky. The fullness of feeling and of connectedness, whether experienced as/through an open window or not, can be freeing and overwhelming – all at once it's awe-inspiring and engulfing.

Given the potential power of feeling (*truly, madly, deeply*), it's no wonder that many institutions appear intent on disciplining and desensitising people. They want us to be disconnected from our interdependent lives and distanced from ourselves too. Contrasting with the numbing messages of many corporate and governmental entities, in *The Book of Delights,*[72] Ross Gay takes readers on a tender journey comprised of a collection of writing on delight in everyday life. What truly makes for delight is not compartmentalising and disconnecting by attempting to numb yourself or others from the realities and harshness of life. Rather, at the core of delight is a delicate dance with a multitude of emotions and sensations, embracing forms of pleasure without doing so being at the expense of engaging with the fuller picture of the world. Put briefly, delights shouldn't involve denial or dismissal of horrors that other beings and the planet face.

Gay's work brings to the fore that experiencing delight doesn't mean disregarding different feelings that are part of the milieu from which delight might manifest – melancholy, uncertainty, heartbreak, and mourning, being among these. Indeed, feeling(s), and expressing such feeling(s), can involve vulnerability. While such vulnerability is not something that everyone is entitled to expect of you, it's part of the conditions that can make connection(s) possible and precious. More than there being strength in softness, there's love in it: a willingness to "put yourself out there", while knowing that in doing so you face the possibility of pain. As we've reflected on, softness has become a synonym for many things. But to us, softness is open heartedness and tender sincerity, even sometimes alongside silliness too. It's embracing others + being embraced, fully and freely.

Softness is not always easy, steady, cushioned, or cute. On the surface, softness might sometimes seem a wee (or even, a lot) bit barbed. There can be softness in the firm way that someone holds you close(r) when you need them to, or in the assertive way that they tell you to be gentle with yourself and to take care. There can be softness in what seems like an abrupt resolve to try do something differently to make amends for hurt caused, or softness in what seems like a brusque exchange, but is really one tinged with the torment of concern and contrition for a loved one. Softness doesn't always present as such – it's not all fluffy clouds, pastel hues, and comforts. Softness can be as demanding as it is dreamy, and that's no bad thing.

No Commands, but (Certain) Demands

"Look, don't touch" is one of countless commanding statements that reflect societal ideas about order, duty, and (dis)connection. There are many times when being told not to touch something or someone is clearly warranted and should be supported, including due to reasons related to safety, sustainability, and self-governance. The action of touch and the intentions behind it are not something inherently "good" and of course aren't something desired by all. Touch can be the cause of harm, such as many forms of physical and sexual abuse, and the erosion and decimation of places. In some situations, the idea of "look, don't touch" – whether uttered or not – may be necessary. But those times shouldn't be confused for moments when messages of "look, don't touch" are just about institutions' attempts to control the behaviours and emotions of people – preventing them/us from connecting with surrounding spaces and all in them.

The last thing we would want is for our book to amount to the suggestion that "look, don't touch" should simply be replaced with other commanding statements. In fact, the river of thoughts and feelings carrying our book includes the idea that to engage with the fullness of feeling(s), and, in turn, life, we need to do away with commands: *commands, be gone* (lol at the irony of this being a command itself).

Wanting the world to be rid of commands is not a radical notion, despite the reticence that it might provoke in some people. A world without commands is possible.

When thinking about what that might look, sound, feel, and be like, some people may fear the possibility of a world free of hierarchies. Depending on your perspective, power, and privilege(s) (or lack thereof), a world free of authorities and structures (e.g. governments and the police) may be a scary and lawless land where hedonism and vigilantism runs riot. Alternatively, such a world is one where collectiveness and communalism flourishes as everyone figures out possibilities without the presence of punitive and paternalistic systems.

This doesn't mean we are advocating for a boundary-less world. Boundaries are an essential part of how care is enacted and are crucial to how connections are conjured. So instead of suggesting that boundaries be thrown out with commands, we're affirming the need for more acknowledgement and nurturing of boundaries in open and conversational ways that move beyond the "being told/scolded" attitude of curt commands and carceral structures.

Now, it might be helpful for us to also reflect on the relationship between demands and connectedness. The terms "commands" and "demands" are often used interchangeably, with both being associated with insistent directives and muzzling mandates. However, there are subtle yet significant differences between them. The root of the word "command" is attributed to the Latin "commandare" which relates to the idea of intensely expressing force. The etymology of "command" has also been outlined as relating to Old French ("commander") which is associated with the idea of authoritatively expressing an order. Given its closeness to the grammars of the military, as well as rank and file approaches (e.g. "commander in chief"), the idea of "commands" seems especially linked to an assumption that society needs a leader (to instill order).

Even though "demand" has similar connotations, it's more marginally linked with the idea of asking (not just telling). Demands, including those made by grassroots movements and people challenging systemic oppression, don't function in the same way as state sanctioned commands. Free Palestine. Free Sudan. Free Congo. End genocide. Kill the Bill. The list goes on. Getting caught up in the specifics of semantics can stymy a focus on meaningful changes, material conditions, and socio-political realities. So, while it's worth distinguishing between commands and demands, it's important not to get so bogged down in these details that we move away from their meanings in practice.

Touching Grass and Wandering/Wondering

Touching grass is an insult associated with people who are deemed so online that they've lost touch with reality and the offline/outside world. To touch grass is to go outside and reconnect with 'realness' and nature. Taking time to touch grass or disconnect becomes increasingly difficult in a world where our dependence on tech is crossed over with the reality that everything is so much more on(line) than it was pre-pandemic.

To dander and wander, ramble and roam across open countryside – despite *everyone* having the statutory rights and freedom to do so in the UK – becomes the reserve of people whose (solo) presence would be unlikely to disrupt narratives about who belongs oot there, and under what conditions. Collective or community-based activities like curated "wellness retreats" often require payment, suggesting that true rest or connection with nature is something which must be bought and embarked upon in a structured way. This approach risks turning even the act of disconnecting into something that only those with resources can afford. This can contribute to the feeling that rest is something designed and controlled by others, not something that arises naturally from within. It forces people to seek alternatives online, adding more digital stimuli instead of genuine disconnection.

Touching grass, then, is for those who can choose (and, usually, afford) time, space and isolation to adopt a slower pace of life, thus creating conditions to thrive beyond highly stimulating manufactured environments.

Sometimes however, the grass isn't greener. For many, the offline outside world can feel like a place of unbelonging. Less accessible, warm and welcoming as a home space than what's been found online. Or maybe there is no grass to touch at all. Sometimes, being able to quickly find a quiet, natural space to just be, might not be possible. With cities (and ever increasingly, areas outwith city boundaries) lacking green public spaces which don't require a financial transaction, the outdoors can feel more like a commodity than a freely available resource. This can lead to a sense of disconnection and can make it harder for people to find peace.

Sometimes, being able to just *be* is impossible and in a chaotic and activating world, perhaps touching grass can be simply about remembering what joy, contentedness and calm feels like – whether inside and online or outside and offline.

There's always lots to wander/wonder aboot. While we've spent time here reflecting on ideas and experiences related to looking (and being looked at) and touching (and being touched), doing so has also meant wandering/

wondering about other things, including many matters that haven't made their way to these pages. After all, part of the freedom to feel can be the freedom from being forced to express. And part of freedom, period, is space to make decisions that are not simply dictated by others' expectations of what you do (not) say and share.

(Wild)Flowers and Wolves

In the early 2000s, the song "Flowers in the Window" (2001) by Scottish band Travis found its way to you in many places. From cafes and shops to hallways and pubs, its message and melody met people where they were, including lyrics about feeling "bad", "sad", "mad", and both loving and being loved – watching flowers grow, together. As the song suggests, "Flowers in the Window" are a sense of blooming – the sweetness and scents of love, including the growth and gloriousness within that. Flowers in the window aren't just ornamental or something to be seen. They're testament to forms of planting, persistence, and patience. They're the outcome of many moments of care and doing much more than merely looking at and not touching something. As the song by Travis speaks to, flowers in the window can be reflections of the freedom of feeling – appreciating how flowers in the window might move you, and the movements that are essential to helping flowers (and love) grow.

Is it ever possible to look (connect) without being touched (moved)?

Unlike the planning and placement of flowers in a window, wildflowers are the result of more random and spontaneous occurrences. As their name suggests, wildflowers are linked to an idea of *wildness* – a freedom from the impulses and intentions of people. Contrasting with the more manicured aesthetic that is associated with flowers in windows, wildflowers emerge and develop in ways that are closely connected to the (un)predictable rhythms of the natural environment and all who inhabit it. Even so, people can and do plant the seeds of some "wildflowers" (and attempt to "rewild" spaces), such as by purchasing them and choosing where they grow. This means that despite the wildness that they're known for, some "wildflowers" are now much more managed by people (looked at *and* touched) than simply stemming from serendipity in "the wild". But, as is indicated by our final pause/paws for thought, it's not just people who might look at, touch, smell, feel, and even, taste flowers.

Recent research suggests that "for the first time", Canis simensis (Ethiopian wolves) have been "reported to feed on nectar,"[73] much like bees do. The findings of an article published in the journal *Ecology* outlines how these wolves feed on the nectar of Kniphofia foliosa (Ethiopian red hot poker flowers), meaning that in doing so they may act as pollinators. This challenges assumptions that carnivorous animals don't engage in plant-pollinator interactions. It's also a reminder of the many ways that animals, plants, flowers, and insects are (inter)connected, with there always being many similarities between creatures and their lives, no matter how different they might also be.

When reading about the wolves feeding on nectar, or when looking at the powerful photograph of them doing just that, you might be moved. The thought and image of wolves enjoying feeding on nectar while aiding pollination, and unaware of the world's surprise at this, is touching. So, all that is to say, whether it's reflecting on wildflowers, wolves, or whatever else you come across during your days on this world (and perhaps on others too), we hope you experience forms of the freedom to feel and the feeling(s) of freedom, while finding, reaching for, and embracing each other.

Playlist

Introduction

1. Volcano by Eartheater
2. Beautiful Disaster by Rachel Chinouriri, Sam Dotia
3. Wish You Were Here by Incubus
4. Letters To You by Finch
5. Help I'm Alive by Metric
6. For Sure by American Football
7. The Only Exception by Paramore
8. Grow Old With Me by The Postal Service
9. Soft Spot by JMSN
10. Saturn by SZA
11. Dreaming by Poly Styrene
12. Day Dreaming by Aretha Franklin
13. (This Is) The Dream of Evan and Chan – Live by The Postal Service
14. Dream Song by Nathan Somevi
15. Daydream by Archie Hamilton and Sadie Walker
16. First Impressions by Kele
17. As by Stevie Wonder
18. Rien à prouver by Yseult
19. Thinkin Bout You by Frank Ocean
20. By Your Side by Sade

Chapter 1

21. Three Babies by Sinéad O'Connor
22. Lean On Me by Bill Withers
23. Close To You by Frank Ocean
24. Sleeping In by The Postal Service
25. Crimson and Clover by Joan Jett & The Blackhearts
26. The Love You Want by Sleep Token
27. Nineteen by Hayley Williams
28. Euclid by Sleep Token
29. White Ferrari by Frank Ocean
30. Metamorphosis by Infinity Song
31. Take Off Your Cool (feat. Norah Jones) by Outkast, Norah Jones
32. Spin Another Web by brownbear
33. It Takes Blood And Guts To Be This Cool But I'm Still Just A Cliché by Skunk Anansie
34. Delilah the Spider (No Beginnings) by Delilah Holliday
35. I'M FINE! I'M GOOD! I'M PERFECT! by SPIDER
36. AMERICA'S NEXT TOP MODEL by SPIDER
37. Celebration Song by Holding Absence
38. 23 by Jimmy Eat World
39. The Coin-Op Guillotine by Los Campesinos!
40. Time Will Tell by Blood Orange
41. Just Pretend (Live 2024) by Bad Omens
42. Kissing Families by Silversun Pickups
43. Talkin' Bout a Revolution by Tracy Chapman
44. Baby Can I Hold You by Tracy Chapman
45. ALIEN LOVE CALL by Turnstile, Blood Orange
46. ATliens by Outkast
47. holdin' on by Zack Fox
48. A Voice note: Sad Boys Club by LEMFRECK
49. So Here We Are (Four Tet Remix) by Bloc Party

50. Teardrop by Massive Attack, Elizabeth Fraser
51. It's Okay To Cry by SOPHIE
52. Tears by TAAHLIAH, Lady Neptune
53. Don't Cry – It's Only The Rhythm by Grace Jones
54. Crying by TV On the Radio
55. Uptown Babies Don't Cry by Max Romeo & The Upsetters
56. Cry by Cigarettes After Sex
57. When Doves Cry by Prince
58. You Know I Should Be Leaving Soon by Yvette Young
59. Uncomfortably Numb (feat. Hayley Williams) by American Football, Hayley Williams
60. Woke Up This Morning by Alabama 3
61. Krwlng (Mike Shinoda Reanimation, featuring Aaron Lewis) by Linkin Park
62. Everybody Hurts by R.E.M.
63. Twilight Galaxy by Metric
64. Intro by Ms. Lauryn Hill
65. Nightcrawler by Aye Nako
66. Dream Big by Bob Vylan
67. I Am Me by Willow Smith [WILLOW]
68. If I Ruled the World (Imagine That) (featuring Lauryn Hill) by Nas

Chapter 2

69. The Chemicals Between Us by Bush
70. Advice by Christy Ogbah
71. I'm Not Okay (I Promise) by My Chemical Romance
72. STOP HURTING MY FEELINGS by LEILAH
73. BE OK by Samoht
74. fine (maybe) by shiv
75. Are You Really Okay? by Sleep Token

76. Don't Give Up by Peter Gabriel feat. Kate Bush
77. Get Yourself Together by Daniel Johnston
78. Don't Wish Me Well by Solange
79. Every You Every Me by Placebo
80. Freefall (featuring Durand Bernarr) by KAYTRANADA
81. Learn To Swim Part II by Joshua Idehen
82. Love Is Overtaking Me by Arthur Russell
83. A Psychic Wound (A Cosmic Cheque version) by Los Campesinos!
84. Velvet Rope by Janet Jackson
85. Snooze by SZA
86. Blue Light (Engineers Anti Gravity Mix) by Bloc Party
87. Wild Ride by MOTHXR
88. I Didn't Know It Was A Gift by Daniel Hart
89. The Whole World Was Ready To Return by Daniel Hart
90. Is It Really You? by Loathe
91. WOOSAH by Dean Blunt
92. PUNK by Dean Blunt
93. Vampires Will Never Hurt You by My Chemical Romance
94. Plans by Bloc Party
95. On by Bloc Party
96. Always by Yvette Young
97. What It Is to Burn by Finch
98. Disarm by The Smashing Pumpkins
99. Foster Nosferatu by Your Arms Are My Cocoon
100. Snowy! by Yours Arms Are My Cocoon
101. I Go Weak by Carroll Thompson
102. In My View by Young Fathers
103. Adieu by Enter Shikari
104. Ohio is for Lovers (Lo-Fi) by Hawthorne Heights / Less Gravity & Aleks!

Chapter 3

105. Humble As The Sun by Bob Vylan, JERUB
106. Everybody Loves The Sunshine by Roy Ayers Ubiquity
107. Without A Song by The Supremes
108. In Circles by Sunny Day Real Estate
109. Hold Me, Thrill Me, Kiss Me by Mel Carter
110. Ain't No Mountain High Enough by Diana Ross
111. COMING FOR UR <3 by LAMAYA
112. Heartbeat by War
113. Black Boys on Mopeds by Sinéad O'Connor
114. Never Meant by American Football
115. Enfys Yn Y Glaw by Kizzy Crawford
116. Blue Moon by Billie Holiday
117. How High the Moon by Ella Fitzgerald
118. Moon River by Frank Ocean
119. Waiting for the Moon to Rise by Belle and Sebastian
120. Darkness by Rage Against The Machine
121. More Than A Woman by Aaliyah
122. Bleed All Over Me by Willow Smith [WILLOW]
123. Rise by Bad Brains
124. Banned in D.C. by Bad Brains
125. Disparate Youth by Santigold
126. Peace And Unity by Lady Hany
127. Stand for Something by Skindred
128. Between Angels and Insects by Papa Roach
129. Change (In the House of Flies) by Deftones
130. Cobra (Rock Remix) [featuring Spiritbox] by Megan Thee Stallion
131. Anxiety by Megan Thee Stallion
132. You Gotta Be ('99 Mix) by Des'ree

Chapter 4

133. Come as You Are by Nirvana
134. Xen by Northlane
135. Art-I-Ficial by Poly Styrene
136. Fremd im eigenen Land by Advanced Chemistry
137. Colonial Mentality by Fela Kuti
138. BLACKOUT by Turnstile
139. Hold The Mirror (Songs For Survival) by Heir of The Cursed
140. Lonely Day by System of a Down
141. Heaven or Las Vegas by Cocteau Twins
142. Storytelling by Funeral for a Friend
143. Beach Song by Leonie Biney
144. Dancing In The Street by Martha and the Vandellas
145. Emily by From First to Last
146. Blood Sweat Fears an introduction by LEMFRECK
147. Apartheid is Nazism by Alpha Blondy
148. Redemption Song by Bob Marley
149. Sketch For Summer by The Durutti Column
150. Some Things Last A Long Time by Daniel Johnston
151. Empire featuring Sinead O'Connor and Benjamin Zephaniah
152. Natural Anthem (Live) by The Postal Service
153. Everything is romantic featuring caroline polachek by Charli xcx
154. Bird So Bad by Moonchild Sanelly

Chapter 5

155. I Still Remember by Bloc Party / This Modern Love (Dave P. and Adam Sparkle's Making Time Remix) by Bloc Party
156. I Feel Love by Donna Summer
157. Friday Afternoons, Op. 7: A New Year Carol (Part 2) by Trent Reznor and Atticus Ross

158. Heatwave by The Blue Nile
159. 4 Degrees by Anohni
160. St. Chroma by Tyler, the Creator (featuring Daniel Caesar)
161. James Joint by Durand Bernarr
162. Wake Up Call by Hawthorne Heights
163. Passenger Seat by Death Cab for Cutie
164. Always New Depths by Bloc Party
165. Swim Good by Frank Ocean / Pink + White by Frank Ocean
166. Digital Bath by Deftones
167. Tech Romance by Her Space Holiday
168. Everybody's Free (To Feel Good) by Quindon Tarver
169. Flowers In The Window by Travis
170. Tulips by Bloc Party
171. All The Birds by Snakeskin, Julia Sabra and Fadi Tabbal
172. Just Like Honey by Jesus and the Mary Chain
173. Thank you by Charlotte Adigéry and Bolis Pupul
174. Creature (Perfect) by Ibeyi

References

Chapter 1

1. Laina Dawes, *What Are You Doing Here?: A Black Woman's Life and Liberation in Heavy Metal*, Bazillion Points, 2012, p. 48.
2. Nate Powell, *Fall Through*, Abrams ComicArts, p. 59.
3. "SPIDER gets shameless", Mia Hughes, *Alternative Press*, 5 July 2024. altpress.com/spider-an-object-of-desire-interview. Accessed 7 October 2024.
4. E.B. White, *Charlotte's Web*, Harper & Brothers, 1952.
5. Joy White, *Like Lockdown Never Happened: Music and Culture During COVID*, Repeater, 2024, pp. 4–5.
6. Vanessa Angélica Villarreal, *Magical/Realism: Essays on Music, Memory, Fantasy, and Borders*, Tiny Reparations Books, 2024, p. 91.
7. Ibid, p. 170.
8. There has been extensive work on speciesism and ways to collectively address it. This includes the work of Aiyana Goodfellow (2021), such as writing on *Radical Companionship: Rejecting Pethood and Embracing Our Multispecies World*, which "speaks of reimagined relations between species" and "is a guide to unlearning the oppressive tendencies within all of us".
9. Joy White, *Like Lockdown Never Happened: Music and Culture During COVID*, Repeater, 2024, p. 6.
10. The concept of "active listening" is one that usually focuses on the experiences of people who can hear. Our use of the term reflects its association with popular concepts of "holding space", but our own interpretation of "active listening" is inclusive of a wide range of senses and forms of communication, not just those with an auditory element. Similarly, our use of the term "look(ing)" is in reference to much more than just visual and sight-based experiences. Instead, our use of both these expressions relates to various forms of interaction, communication, sensing, and existing in relation to others around you. Relatedly, we recommend reading the 2023 book *On Cuddling: Loved to Death in the Racial Embrace* by Phanuel Antwi.

Chapter 2

11 Gemma June Howell (ed), *Land of Change: Stories of Struggle & Solidarity from Wales*, Culture Matters, 2022, p. 8.

12 During the last stretch of writing our book, the UK's Museum of Youth Culture launched an exhibition titled "I'm Not Okay (an Emo Retrospective)" at the Barbican Music Library in London. For more information about the exhibition and its tribute to noughties emo and related Y2K digital culture: museumofyouthculture.com/im-not-okay.

13 Lama Rod Owens, *Love and Rage: The Path of Liberation Through Anger*, North Atlantic Books, 2020.

14 "Our Mission", Head Above The Waves. hatw.co.uk/about-us/our-mission. Accessed 7 October 2024.

15 Daniel Lukes and Stanimir Panayotov (eds), *black metal rainbows*, PM Press, 2023, p. 13.

16 Audrey Niffeneggar "Interview with the Vampire: An Appreciation", in Anne Rice, *Interview with the Vampire*, 2008, p. 3.

17 Maryam Jameela, "The (Un)Changing Nature of Constructions of South Asian Muslim Women Post 9/11" PhD Thesis, University of Sheffield, 2020. etheses.whiterose.ac.uk/26026. Accessed 7 October 2024, pp. 127–128.

18 George A. Dunn and Rebecca Housel (eds), *True Blood and Philosophy: We Wanna Think Bad Things with You*, John Wiley & Sons, 2010.

19 VampireFreaks (aka vampirefreaks.com) is a website once known for being a social networking site aimed at goths and goth-adjacent subcultures. It's helpful to turn to Chris Brickley's explanation of the term "goth" in the brilliant 2024 book *Heartlands: The Original Goth Scene in Scotland*, "The 'G' word is a useful and familiar generic term, nothing more. Endearing to some, embraced by many. Rejected by more. In popular culture it's now a pejorative term, or at least a crutch for humour" (p. 5). Launched in 1999, the VampireFreaks site has homed a clothing store since 2001. The removal of its social network element occurred in 2020.

20 Andrew Keahey, "We Deserve to See More Black Vampires on the Screen", *The Black Youth Project*, 20 February 2019.

blackyouthproject.com/we-deserve-to-see-more-black-vampires-on-the-screen. Accessed 7 October 2024.
21 Robin R. Means Coleman and Mark H. Harris, *The Black Guy Dies First: Black Horror Cinema from Fodder to Oscar*, S&S/Saga Press, 2023.
22 Melanie McFarland, "Beware the rise of vampire shows. It could mean a recession is looming", *salon*, 23 October 2022. salon.com/2022/10/23/vampire-shows-recession-economy. Accessed 7 October 2024.

Chapter 3

23 Andre Paine, "Vinyl sales increase again with growth accelerating in 2023", *Music Week*, 28 December 2023. musicweek.com/labels/read/vinyl-sales-increase-again-with-growth-accelerating-in-2023/089042. Accessed 7 October 2024.
24 Keith Caulfield, "U.S. Vinyl Album Sales Rise for 17th Straight Year — But Growth Is Slowing", *billboard*, 1 November 2023. billboard.com/pro/vinyl-album-sales-rise-growth-slowing/. Accessed 7 October 2024.
25 Becky Buckle, "UK vinyl sales hit highest level since 1990", *Mixmag*, 3 January 2024. mixmag.net/read/uk-vinyl-sales-reach-its-highest-level-since-1990-news. Accessed 16 December 2024.
26 Charlotte Krol, "Study finds 50 per cent of vinyl buyers in US don't have a record player", *NME*, 29 April 2023. nme.com/news/music/study-finds-50-per-cent-of-vinyl-buyers-in-us-dont-have-a-record-player-3437301. Accessed 16 December 2024.
27 Jenessa Williams, "Tracing Music Fandom Practice Through The Internet", *Museum of Youth Culture*, 1 September 2023. museumofyouthculture.com/tracing-music-fandom-practice-through-the-internet. Accessed 16 December 2024.
28 Joy White, *Like Lockdown Never Happened: Music and Culture During COVID*, Repeater, 2024, p. 2.
29 Other examples of dogs being treated as means to an end, and in ways that are much more perilous than them posthumously modelling for paintings, include the experiences of

the dogs Laika, Belka, and Strelka. These dogs were sent to outer space as "Soviet Space Dogs" in the 1950s and 1960s, with Laika (launched into space in 1957) – a husky-terrier mix – being picked from the streets of Moscow, and only Belka and Strelka returning from space alive in 1960. More information about the lives of these dogs and the Soviet space programme that they were part of is available in the book *Soviet Space Dogs* by Olesya Turkina (2014).

30 On March 19, 1993, Brandon Lee met with interviewer Ira Teller on the set of *The Crow* (1994). This would end up being Lee's last known recorded interview before his death. Footage from the interview can be viewed on YouTube: youtube.com/watch?v=lzKDxQUVE5U.

31 Dele Fadele "Metallica: Masters Of What?", *New Musical Express*, 21 March 1987. rocksbackpages.com/Library/Article/metallica-masters-of-what. Accessed 7 October 2024.

32 Chris L. Terry, "Beyond Bad Brains". In James Spooner and Chris L. Terry (eds), *Black Punk Now: Fiction, Non-fiction and Comics*, Soft Skull Press, 2023, p. 6.

33 "Santigold: Tiny Desk Concert", *NPR Music*, 21 November 2022: youtube.com/watch?v=IG76Rf28MQA.

34 Moya Bailey, "They aren't talking about me…", *The Crunk Feminist Collective*, 14 March 2010. crunkfeministcollective.com/2010/03/14/they-arent-talking-about-me. Accessed 7 October 2024.

35 Moya Bailey and Trudy, "On misogynoir: citation, erasure, and plagiarism", *Feminist Media Studies* 18(4): 762–768, 2018.

36 bell hooks, *Black Looks: Race and Representation*, Routledge, 2014.

37 George Garner, "Spiritbox on their first Grammy nomination, collaborating with Megan Thee Stallion & more", *Music Week*, 14 December 2023. musicweek.com/talent/read/spiritbox-on-their-first-grammy-nomination-collaborating-with-megan-thee-stallion-more/089011. Accessed 7 October 2024.

38 Maureen Mahon, *Black Diamond Queens: African American Women and Rock and Roll*, 2020. Duke University Press, p. 2.

39 Philip Trapp, "Megan Thee Stallion Vamps to Static-X Song

On Instagram, Band + Fans React", *Loudwire*, 6 February 2024. lloudwire.com/megan-thee-stallion-static-x-song-video-reactions/#:~:text=In%20Megan%27s%20Instagram%20comments%2C%20some,Static-X%20bandleader%20Wayne%20Static.. Accessed 7 October 2024.

40 Ibid.

41 @theestallion, "No but thee hotties seem to like it so I might need to tune in lol #HOTGIRLVMAS". x.com/theestallion/status/1830701007229137337, 2 September 2024. Accessed 7 October 2024.

42 Jenessa Williams, "Tracing Music Fandom Practice Through The Internet", *Museum of Youth Culture*, 1 September 2023. museumofyouthculture.com/tracing-music-fandom-practice-through-the-internet. Accessed 16 December 2024.

43 Arusa Qureshi, *Flip the Script: How Women Came to Rule Hip Hop*. 404 Ink, 2021.

44 Craig Reynolds (@reynlord), "how do sub genre names stick? like djent and nu metal etc? because i got one that i call bands like sleep token, bad omens and spiritbox. baddiecore. metalcore with enough pop music crossover and sex appeal that normie hot people like it", *X*, 18 August 2023. x.com/reynlord/status/1692524508320579677. Accessed 7 October 2024.

45 "Yacht Rock" is a term that has been used in relation to a broad range and styles of music linked to soft rock, as well as expressions of smooth soul, R&B, jazz, and disco. Having become prominent and commercially successful from the mid-1970s to mid-1980s, such music became associated with the label "Yacht Rock" much more recently, as the descriptive term didn't appear and gain traction until 2005, following on from an online mockumentary style video series titled "Yacht Rock" (2005–2010). HBO's *Yacht Rock: A Dockumentary* (2024) provides an account of some of the defining moments in the history of such music.

46 Maureen Mahon, *Black Diamond Queens: African American Women and Rock and Roll*, Duke University Press, 2020, p. 1.

47 Laina Dawes, *What Are You Doing Here?: A Black Woman's Life and Liberation in Heavy Metal*, Bazillion Points, 2012, p. 49.

48 More information about use of the term "un-alived" in Seattle's Museum of Pop Culture exhibition is available in Ashley Iasimone's 2024 *Billboard* article: billboard.com/music/music-news/kurt-cobain-unalived-nirvana-exhibit-seattle-museum-pop-culture-1235750842. Accessed 16 December 2024.

Chapter 4

49 Ione Gamble, *Poor Little Sick Girls: A love letter to unacceptable women*, Dialogue, 2022, p. 10.
50 NHS under pressure – Scotland: bma.org.uk/advice-and-support/nhs-delivery-and-workforce/pressures/nhs-under-pressure-scotland and Health funding data analysis: bma.org.uk/advice-and-support/nhs-delivery-and-workforce/funding/health-funding-data-analysis. Accessed 19 October 2024.
51 The Workers' Stories Project: facebook.com/WorkersStories/
52 Bob Vylan, "The British government don't care about the arts" from *101 Part Time Jobs with Giles Bidder*. everand.com/listen/podcast/721353961. Accessed 16 December 2024.
53 The Moon, "THANK YOU FROM THE MOON", *The Moon*, 22 November 2024. themooncardiff.com. Accessed 22 November 2024.
54 "Cardiff Just Lost Key Alt Venue The Moon; The City Responds", *Clash*, 26 November 2024. clashmusic.com/features/cardiff-just-lost-key-alt-venue-the-moon-the-city-responds. Accessed 26 November 2024.
55 The Hip-Hop Radio Archive is an incredible online resource which "aims to digitize, preserve, share, and contextualize recordings of hip-hop radio from the 1980s and 1990s from commercial, college, community, and pirate stations of all sizes, telling the stories of the shows and the people that made them." hiphopradioarchive.org.
56 The *Now That's What I Call Music* website shows expansion into K-pop, Pride, Halloween and a clothing line. There is even a "Now That's What I Call Hip-Hop at 50".
57 More details on Chalkpit Cassette Club here:

58 Kate Lindsay, "Who's Afraid of These Gen Alpha Queens?", *Bustle*, 31 October 2024. bustle.com/life/gen-alpha-tiktok-social-media-teachers-afraid. Accessed 1 November 2024.

59 bell hooks, *Yearning: Race, Gender, and Cultural Politics*, Routledge, 2015.

60 To learn more about jewellery, culture, and identity, we recommend reading the 2023 book *The Nameplate* by Isabel Attyah Flower and Marcel Rosa-Salas. For more on Glossier in *Fortune* (2020): fortune.com/2020/08/18/glossier-black-workers-donation-support-black-lives-ceo-emily-weiss/amp/ and an example of clean girl aesthetic by Glossier CEO and founder in *In the Gloss* (2016): intothegloss.com/2016/02/emily-weiss-wedding-beauty/. Accessed 3 October 2024.

61 This became a trending term online, following on from the viral video content of creator Jools Lebron, a Cuban trans woman who eventually took legal action after somebody attempted to copyright the expression in the days after its initial online popularity.

62 The phrase hot girl summer was initially shared on X by Megan Thee Stallion in 2018.

63 Ashley C. Ford, "Don't Mess With Megan", *The Cut*, 29 August 2022. thecut.com/article/megan-thee-stallion-traumazine-profile.html. Accessed 9 October 2024.

64 Bad Bitches Have Bad Days Too: badbitcheshavebaddaystoo.com. Accessed 1 November 2024.

65 "brat" in Collins Online Dictionary: collinsdictionary.com/dictionary/english/brat.

66 Cat Zhang, "Breaking Down Charli XCX's *Brat* Remix Lineup", *The Cut*, 7 October 2024. thecut.com/article/breaking-down-charli-xcxs-brat-remix-album-track-by-track.html. Accessed 9 October 2024.

67 Charli xcx (7 June, 2024) on Instagram: instagram.com/charli_xcx/p/C77frc7gy_y/?hl=en. Accessed 9 October 2024.

68 Ismatu Gwendolyn, "There is no safety in being Beautiful: reflections from a life spent On Display™", *Threadings*, 10 August 2023. ismatu.substack.com/p/24-there-is-no-safety-in-being-beautiful. Accessed 1 December 2024.

Conclusion

69 Abdulkreem Al-Juhani, Muhammad Imran, Zeyad K Aljaili, Meshal M Alzhrani, Rawan A Alsalman, Marwah Ahmed, Dana K Ali, Mutaz I Fallatah, Hamad M Yousuf, and Leena M Dajan, "Beyond the Pump: A Narrative Study Exploring Heart Memory", *Cureus* 30;16(4): e59385, 2024. pubmed.ncbi.nlm.nih.gov/38694651/. Accessed 7 October 2024.

70 A line from William Shakespeare's (1594–1597) play "Romeo and Juliet", spoken by Romeo in Act 2, Scene 2.

71 Such statements are spoken by Bonita Smith (Tyler, the Creator's mother) as the opening to the song St. Chroma by Tyler, the Creator (featuring Daniel Caesar).

72 Ross Gay, *The Book of Delights*, Hatchette, 2022.

73 Sandra Lai, Don-Jean Léandri-Breton, Adrien Lesaffre, Abdi Samune, Jorgelina Marino, and Claudio Sillero-Zubiri, "Canids as pollinators? Nectar foraging by Ethiopian wolves may contribute to the pollination of *Kniphofia foliosa*", *Ecology*, 2024.

Acknowledgements

cesca, my sister. for sharing your <3, dreams + patience with me in this + in life. i love + appreciate you. xx

j, for liking saft rolls oan a sunday. foxi, woof woof woof. buuuuurrrrrrrrrp. wagwagwagwagwag (thank you for showing me how to be more fully (especially yawns).

even with all that seasons bring, being climbed + crawled upon, pecked at, shaken, bits broken + torn off, a tree might change, but still remains a tree. be rooted to + savour your feelings.

layla, with love and appreciation for all of who you are <3, the ways we wonder/wander, so many different journeys together, and times spent chatting and chuckling over tasty things/brews, on phone calls or over messages, and while on everyday adventures. xx

To all fam, far, near, but always so very dear <3

Ez, for your whiskeriness and spiritedness, as well as your embrace of excitement, ease, curiosity, love, and openness, all while snuffling, tasting, snoozing, and snuggling your way through the days. <3

To those who seem as though they've always been (t)here, no matter when you meet <3

Heather and Laura for all your support. This book wouldn't have been possible without your encouragement and guidance, or without you both understanding what and how we wanted to write and share this work.

When we feel, we live and remember those who have lived.

When we feel, we love and remember those who have loved.

About the Authors

layla-roxanne hill is an independent writer, researcher + organiser. she thinks + feels about many things, including class, anti-colonial struggle, care + belonging + the way our conditions move us to act. layla-roxanne is co-author/dreamer with francesca sobande of *Black Oot Here: Black Lives in Scotland*. she is active in the trade union movement, holding elected positions within the bureaucratic machinery. layla-roxanne likes rabbit holes, finding peace + connection + to lift heavy.

Francesca Sobande is a writer and reader in digital media studies, who lives in Cymru (Wales). She is co-author/co-dreamer with layla-roxanne hill of *Black Oot Here: Black Lives in Scotland*. Her bylines include *Disegno*, *Paste Magazine*, and *The Vinyl Factory*. Francesca enjoys midnight skies and all things emo <3

About the Inklings series

This book is part of 404 Ink's Inkling series which presents big ideas in pocket-sized books.

They are all available at 404ink.com/shop.

If you enjoyed this book, you may also enjoy these titles in the series:

Revolutionary Desires – Xuanlin Tham

Cinema is becoming less and less sexy; yet more and more people are rallying against sex on screen. Why is the sex scene, demonised as it is, therefore more politically important and subversive than ever? *Revolutionary Desires* seeks to answer that question.

Roses for Hedone – Prishita Maheshwari-Aplin

As we face ongoing and new challenges to creating a fairer world, let us borrow from the Ancient Greeks' understanding of love's multiplicity to explore queer hedonism not as a momentary phenomenon, but rather a transformational route through which we can learn from our past, connect in the present, and look towards the future with hope – together.